Living Simply, Giving Generously

A Biography of David and Jeannie Byer

Living Simply, Giving Generously

A Biography of David and Jeannie Byer

By E. Morris Sider

Published by
The Brethren in Christ Historical Society
Sponsored by
The Friends of Murray Library, Messiah College

Also by the Author

Fire in the Mountains: The Story of a Revival Movement in Central Pennsylvania

A Vision for Service: A History of Upland College

Nine Portraits: Brethren in Christ Biographical Sketches

Fruit from Woods and Sands: The Story of Houghton Mission

Lantern in the Dawn: Selections from the Writings of John E. Zercher (ed., with Paul Hostetler).

Here Faith and Learning Meet: The Story of Niagara Christian College

Messenger of Grace: A Biography of C. N. Hostetter, Jr.

Messiah College: A History

More Than Names: A Story of John and Barbara Martin

Holiness Unto the Lord: The Story of Roxbury Holiness Camp

Leader Among Brethren: Biographies of Henry Ginder and Charlie B. Byers

The Brethren in Christ in Canada: Two Hundred Years of Tradition and Change

Called to Evangelism: The Life and Ministry of John L. Rosenberry

A Stewardship of Heritage: History-keeping in the Congregation

My Story, My Song: Life Stories of Brethren in Christ Missionaries (ed.)

Within the Perfection of Christ: Essays on Peace and the Nature of the Church (ed., with Terry Brensinger)

Amazing Grace: My Own Story of Rejection and Redemption (with Shadrack Maloka)

Beyond Our Dreams: The Story of Kenbrook Camp

We Have This Ministry: Pastoral Theory and Practice in the Brethren in Christ Church (ed.)

Preaching the Word: Sermons by Brethren in Christ Ministers (ed.)

Reflections on a Heritage: Defining the Brethren in Christ (ed.)

Canadian Portraits: Brethren in Christ Biographical Sketches

Lives Remembered: Canadian Brethren in Christ Biographical Sketches (ed.)

A Peace Reader (ed., with Luke Keefer, Jr.)

Faithful Witnesses: Canadian Brethren in Christ Biographical Sketches (ed.)

A Home on Paxton Street

Touching Hearts on Shores Worldwide: Sixty Years of Gospel Tide Radio Ministry

Windows to the Church (ed.)

Celebrating Women's Stories (ed., with Rebecca Ebersole and Dorcas Steckbeck)

Celebration: A Centennial History of the Grantham Brethren in Christ

A Living and Growing Ministry: The Story of Roxbury Holiness Camp

Brethren in Christ History and Life (journal, ed., 1978-2013)

Dedication

To all who, like David and Jeannie,
live simply and give generously.

Library of Congress Control Number: 2015951244

Printed in the United States of America

Contents

Introduction

David and Jeannie Byer encouraged people to live simply and give generously. The two parts of this expression are related: live simply in order to give generously.

As this biography attempts to show, the Byers practiced what they preached, although the preaching was more by example than by proclamation. My hope is that this book will serve to spread abroad this principle by which they have lived.

The book is designed to be read in a relatively short time. The chapters are not long; the length of the book is limited. In part, the design is intended to attract readers in an age when long books and lengthy passages are generally out of fashion. The appendices contain various accounts that are significant but omitted in the main text in order to retain the flow of the narrative.

I have limited the documentation of sources. My first thought was to omit all references in order to make the book more attractive to a general audience. But my lifelong career as a historian led me to include at least some references. I have not referenced information given by the Byers either in interviews or by email. Readers should assume that where documentation appears to be lacking, the information comes from the Byers.

Readers may be surprised at David's frank account of his depression in Appendix II. At our first session together, he insisted that his depression, being part of his story, must be told. I agreed. We both also considered that this part of the biography may be helpful to individuals and families who are caught in similar circumstances. Dr. Roger Sider, a psychiatrist, on consultation, encouraged its inclusion in the biography. David's children gave their consent to publish the account. Because of the personal nature of this experience, I asked David to write the account himself. Included in the appendices is Jeannie's tale of the family's trip through Europe in 1988, one of four that they took. I considered the account too long to include in the main text, but one that should be included in the book for its illustrative value. Among other elements of family life, it shows Jeannie's organizational skills, the family's interest in exploring new places and meeting people beyond their Rochester locale, the ability to adjust to unexpected situations, and the humor that pervaded the lives of the parents and children. Because of its length, the original account is somewhat abridged.

I owe thanks to many people for their assistance in producing this book. My debt is greatest to David and Jeannie Byer for hosting me in their home in Rochester, Minnesota, for several days while I interviewed them, and afterwards for the many emails that they sent me in response to questions and requests for further information. My thanks also go to Cherie Fieser, Library Special Projects Administrator and Curator of Book Arts, Messiah College, for her encouragement and for making available the correspondence between her and the Byers relating to the Ruth E. Engle Memorial Collection of Children's Book Illustration.

I received valuable information from family and friends of David and Jeannie. In alphabetical order they are: Steve and Alene Burgert, Leslie Byer, Paul Byer, Lois Byer Caffrey, Mark and Melinda Evinger, Janet Byer Groff, Jerry and Margaret Huebner, Don and Carol Heuton, Eugene and Margaret Hokanson, David and Fran Jordan, Ron and Sheryl Peterson, Elaine Byer Heuton, Steven R. Rettke, Arlene Schuiteman, Peter Southorn, John and Esther Spurrier, and Phyllis Colburn Tucker. Also assisting me were readers of an early draft. They include (also listed alphabetically) Harriet Bicksler, Mike Brown, Jeannie Byer, Cherie Fieser, Janet Groff, Beth Mark, Paul Nisly, and Paul Wengert. I owe thanks also to Bonnie Ganoe and Diane Hunsinger for typing services, to Glen Pierce for formatting the text, and to Morris Sherk for research assistance.

I am grateful to the Brethren in Christ Historical Society for readily agreeing to publish this volume, and to the generous donors who provided financial assistance to make publication possible. Their names are listed on the inside back cover of the book.

I take delight in crediting my wife Leone with her rightful share in producing this biography—for giving me the time, space, and encouragement that all writers wish to have.

E. Morris Sider
Grantham, PA
August 2015

1

Family Heritages

"They walk the walk, and talk the talk." "They live to help others, not themselves." These comments, from two different sources, nicely characterize the subjects of this book, David and Jean Byer. Both accepted the heritage passed on to them; both achieved success in the medical world; both involved themselves in the work of their congregation and missions in Africa. They have given generously to such institutions as Messiah College, and have provided financial aid to students. Admirably woven into these activities is their unostentatious lifestyle. Their advice to "live simply, give generously" comes from their own practice of these virtues.

Surely theirs is a story that should be told.

The Byer Heritage

The Byers trace their ancestry back to the Reformation in sixteenth-century Europe. The Boyers (an early spelling of the name) were part of the Anabaptist movement, a radical element that sought to take the Reformation to its logical conclusion. Anabaptists emphasized such views as brotherhood (community), obedience to biblical commands (especially those of the New Testament), peace, and adult (believers) baptism rather than infant baptism as the means of entry into the church. Such views and practices naturally separated them from the rest of the surrounding religious and social communities. Understandably, such convictions were unacceptable to the authorities—religious and secular—of that time. As a result, Anabaptists were severely persecuted. Persecution forced many Anabaptists to escape from places like Switzerland to more tolerant areas of Europe, especially to the German area of the Palatinate.

Jacob Boehm, one of whose descendants would marry a Byer, was a Swiss Anabaptist who converted from the Reformed Church. Tried, convicted and jailed, he managed, however, to escape to the Palatinate. But when toleration even there seemed threatened, Jacob's son, also named Jacob, immigrated to Pennsylvania probably around 1717 (sources vary) with the large Mennonite influx into the Lancaster County area.

Martin Boehm, one of Jacob's sons, figured significantly in Brethren in Christ history. A Mennonite minister, he experienced a radical conversion in the Pietist manner.[1] With Philip Otterbein he preached in a series of meetings in Lancaster County, Pennsylvania, in which many in the community also received a radical conversion. Among them were the founders of the Brethren in Christ (earlier called River Brethren).

The Revolutionary War was not kind to Mennonites and other peace groups. Abraham Boehm, another of Jacob Boehm's sons and brother to Martin, was among those who suffered. He was accused of aiding the British and heavily fined. "Everything he possessed was sacrificed to the fury of an unnatural rebellion except his life and integrity," according to a source from the period. Another Boehm brother was jailed and fined for not participating in the war against the British.[2]

Such treatment led some Mennonites (and some River Brethren) to move to Upper Canada, now Ontario. Here, they thought, they would be more tolerantly treated under British rule. (The availability of cheap land was also an attraction.)

Abraham Boehm, his wife and son, were among those who immigrated to Upper Canada where they settled in the Niagara area. Around 1797 his sister, widow Anna Byer, who had previously married Martin Boyer/Byer, followed to be near her brother. The Byers owned a significant amount of acreage along the Niagara River a few miles north of Fort Erie and close to the present Niagara Christian Collegiate (a Brethren in Christ high school).

With Anna came two daughters and one son, John. Somewhere between 1852 and 1861 they became Brethren in Christ (then known as Tunkers) and joined the group who had earlier moved to the area.

In 1866, to obtain better land, son John moved to the Markham vicinity a few miles north of Toronto. Here the family became members of the Heise Hill congregation established early in the century. John's son, also named John, married Anna Heise of the Heise Hill congregation.[3]

But once again the Byers were on the move, this time to Brown County, Kansas. In 1872, Christian (Christopher) Heise of the Heise Hill congregation bought land in the county (in the following years he traveled between Ontario and Brown County). Two years later, in 1874, Ben Byer (grandson of Anna who had immigrated to Ontario) followed Christian Heise to Brown County. They were part of the movement to Kansas of Brethren in Christ from Pennsylvania and Ontario, although most Brethren in Christ settled in the Abilene, Dickinson County, area.[4]

Other Brethren in Christ from Pennsylvania and Ontario joined the Byer family in Brown County, including Christian's son Anthony. They came together in their homes for worship; in 1882 they constructed a church which they named Pleasant Hill. By 1900 the congregation numbered around 100 members, although in the following years that number gradually decreased owing to members moving elsewhere.

Levi Byer, the grandfather of David Byer, arrived in Brown County in 1884 as the two-month-old baby son of John Henry and Anna (daughter of Christopher Heise) Byer. Levi became an excellent farmer; he accepted modern farming methods and reaped good financial rewards for his work. He was highly respected in the community, where he was a member of the local school board (an exception to Brethren in Christ views on holding "worldly" offices), and in the Pleasant Hill congregation.

Obituaries, then and now, are noted for their overriding positive statements on the deceased person's life. Even recognizing this characteristic in Levi's obituary, the sentiments expressed are indicative of his being a good man. The long obituary in a local newspaper reads, in part: "He was highly regarded.... His counsel was solicited and highly valued by his fellowman. Through helpfulness and good will, together with honorable business principles, he won many friends." His obituary in the *Evangelical Visitor*, the denomination's official publication, described Levi as "a kind husband, father and brother, concerned for the spiritual welfare of his children; religious and educational opportunities were given generous consideration. He was much interested in advancing the Foreign Mission work of the church."[5]

Levi married Mary Book of Kansas (originally of Iowa). The couple had five sons and two daughters, in order of birth, Glen, Lois, Everett, Verland, Wendel, Donald, and Carol.

When Levi died in 1935 at the age of fifty-one, he left his wife with most of their children still at home and still in their teenage years. To make matters worse for the family, the Great Depression had still not lifted. But with the help of her children and by running a "tight ship," Mary and her family survived. Eventually she accumulated a "nest egg," as one of her sons remarked. In the early 1940s, with nest egg in hand, she retired to California where some of her relatives lived. She died there in 1970.[6]

Everett Byer

The third of Levi and Mary's children, Everett (the father of David) was born in 1912. At the age of eight he was converted; three years later he was baptized and became a member of the Pleasant Hill congregation.

From his childhood, Everett was frugal yet generous. When he was eleven he inherited $100 from his great-aunt, Mary Ann Byer, which he deposited in the Morrill Bank. Every year he collected the $5.00 interest on the account, using the money to buy simple gifts for his brothers and sisters at Christmas.

Everett hoped to obtain an education beyond high school. With this intent, he entered Beulah (later Upland) College in California in 1931. After a year there, he stayed home for a year because of the Depression. In 1933, he again returned to California and attended Beulah College, working evenings and Saturdays to earn money to pay expenses. Here, according to the college yearbook, he impressed fellow students as being "persevering, sure, conscientious, scientific in every way, even to the choice of words." At the end of the school year, however, Everett went back to Kansas and did not return to Beulah College. In the fall of 1934, Everett enrolled in Taylor University in Indiana. Taylor had offered him a scholarship that involved washing dishes in the kitchen and doing maintenance work on the campus. He applied himself well to his studies and manual labor, as suggested by his words in the caption connected with his photograph in the school's student yearbook: "For me, life is a strenuous thing." On March 10, 1935, Everett returned home to visit his parents, who were both ill. He did not return to college that spring, but helped at home. His father died on May 15, 1935. Everett stayed at home another year and worked on the farm.

Back home again in Kansas he began to think about becoming a missionary, perhaps a medical missionary because in those years the Brethren in Christ were beginning to understand the value of medical work accompanying mission work. At one point in these years the Foreign Mission Board interviewed him as a prospective missionary. With medical mission work in mind, he entered Kansas University in September 1936, but he soon discovered that he was too far behind in his studies, especially in chemistry, to become a medical doctor. His college career ended in May 1937.

These educational experiences, each of them short, finally persuaded Everett to be a Kansas farmer. In later years he would say, "I set out to be the best farmer I could be." In this determination he was successful.

Although he did not become a missionary, Everett remained much interested in the work of the church. After World War II, along with men from other peace churches, he worked on a boat shipping cattle to Europe as part of a relief program. In 1964 he went to Alaska with Mennonite Disaster Service to help rebuild the area struck by the earthquake of that year. As will be noted, he and his wife made several trips to Africa to visit Brethren in Christ missions. Through the years they gave generously of their finances to the work of missions.

Adela Tissot

Jules and Jennie Van Camp Tissot, David's maternal great-grandparents, in 1884 emigrated from Switzerland to the United States where they settled on a farm in Nebraska. After the death of his wife, Jules remarried and the couple moved to near Chino in California. Here he and his son Arthur farmed together and together joined the Chino Brethren in Christ Church. In 1912, Arthur married Lucy Violet Williams. The couple had five daughters, of whom the oldest was Adela, Everett's future wife.

Everett had already met the Tissot family and his future wife. In 1933, while he was attending Beulah College, he worked on the Tissot farm. He later described this relatively short time with the Tissots: "I was offered a job helping to fill silo for a Chino dairyman, Arthur Tissot. There for the first time I met his five delightful daughters…. I was most favorably impressed by the quality and character of the family." The Tissot daughters, especially Adela, were a major factor in returning to California to study at Beulah College. Everett liked to say that he "went to California to introduce new genes, new blood into the Brethren in Christ Church," so he married a Tissot.

Adela was a bright and attractive young woman. She too attended Beulah College; they were students together in the 1933-1934 school year. The college yearbook (*The*

Echo) described her as "quiet, brilliant and studious and ever ready to say 'I'll try.'"[7]

Following graduation from Beulah College, Adela enrolled in the Huntington Memorial School of Nursing (attended by other Brethren in Christ young women) from which she graduated in 1939. Marriage to Everett in 1940, however, ended her nursing career, except much later in life when she worked in the Hiawatha (Kansas) Community Hospital.

Everett and Adela had four children—Ruth (who died in infancy), David (of this biography), Janet, and Leslie (Les).

The Jordan Heritage

Jeannie Jordan, who became David's wife, was a descendant on her mother's side of Scottish Presbyterians. These ancestors, the McClures, in earlier years fled to Ireland to escape oppression by the established Anglican Church. Because of the potato famine in the mid-nineteenth century, the McClures immigrated to Pennsylvania. A family story relates that one member of the family supposedly died while crossing the Atlantic Ocean. But as the ship's crew prepared to throw her overboard, she coughed and survived to safely arrive in the United States.

In this country most of the McClures were preachers or medical doctors. One McClure, Robert, invented a reaper that is now on display in the Henry Ford Museum in Dearborn, Michigan. The McClure house in West Middletown, Pennsylvania, had a secret room in which to hide runaway slaves traveling to Canada on the Underground Railway.

While the background of Mary Alice Criswell (Jeannie's mother) was Presbyterian, her husband's background was Baptist and Church of Christ. After graduating from college, still unknown to each other, both Mary Alice and her future husband worked in Washington, D.C., in the same building. They met when they both rushed to a window to watch an air show.[8]

Charles Jordan had wanted to be a Baptist agricultural missionary in Burma. But he was allergic to quinine, the only medicine available at that time to combat malaria. By the end of World War II, however, other drugs were available to fight the disease. This opened the way for the Jordans to serve in missions overseas. Their opportunity to do so came at the suggestion of a relative, Donald McClure, who told the Jordans of the need for an agriculturist in South Sudan, following the death by a lion of the mission's agriculturist. Accepting this challenge, the Jordans left for South Sudan in 1947, taking with them Jeannie (nearly five years of age) and brothers Jack (three years), and David (six months).

In South Sudan, Charles Jordan taught good farming methods, including how to produce better crops and animals, such as cows and chickens. He introduced citrus and other fruits, beans, tomatoes, sweet potatoes, and a better variety of sorghum and corn—all intended to improve a diet that had been based mainly on sorghum.

Trained as a home economist, Jeannie's mother, among other mission activities and caring for a family, worked in the mission's clinic. She became adept at doing eyelid surgery to correct scar tissue resulting from trachoma.

In 1956, Sudan became an independent nation. The new government gradually forced all missionaries to leave the country. In 1961, instead of returning to the United

States, the Jordans moved their ministry to Ethiopia where they remained until they were evacuated in 1977.

This rich heritage of sacrifice and service from the Byer and Jordan families would significantly affect the lives of David and Jeannie Jordan Byer.

2

Childhood and Youth: David

Earliest Impressions

In some ways, David seems to have had a fairly typical childhood. He liked to talk to his dog and share ice cream cones with it. As most boys do, he delighted in teasing his sister Janet, six years younger. "He was quite a tease and pest," she recalls. "He would chase me with worms telling me they were snakes, come downstairs growling and draped in an old black fur coat, or have some other way of scaring me."[1]

Yet he was proud to have a little sister. When Janet was born, little David went from house to house in the village of Hamlin announcing that he had a baby sister and that her hair was the color of copper. The two children, along with a younger brother, Leslie (Les), played happily together in a sandbox that their father made for them.

Until Janet arrived in the family, David had few other children with whom to play. This meant that his association was largely with adults. But he liked to be with them and to speak their adult language. His mother once wrote that he liked to talk with adults even as a three-year-old child. At the same age, David advised an unknown elderly man that he should stop smoking.

David's activities sometimes led to injuries. One day he and the tire he was rolling ran into a hog coop that his father was moving with his tractor. David's leg was broken in three places. His mother thought he might never walk normally again, but he did. One time when he and another boy were racing down a curving hill on their bicycles, David lost control of his bicycle and landed in the ditch, suffering a concussion. When he was fourteen, he attended the 4-H club fair with his heifer; overnight while he was sleeping something made a large gash on his head, possibly the animal.

David early showed an inquisitive mind. Janet recalls that he always seemed to have his nose in a book, and he sometimes became so absorbed with his reading that he did not hear his mother when she called him to do something. Sometimes at night when the light in his room should have been out, he was caught under the bed covers reading a book by flashlight.

His interests were many and varied. He participated in many activities—stamp collecting, youth group programs, Bible quizzing, and 4-H projects among them.

His greatest interest was in science-related subjects, including health, chemistry, and biology. He purchased books in these areas and studied them at home. He once came home with a rabbit he had shot. He and Janet dissected it in the basement.

High School Activities

In high school, these interests and his growing knowledge of them led the mathematics teacher to encourage him to attend two summer camps in science and mathematics conducted by the University of Kansas. The experiences of these two camps were a factor in his decision to go to medical school.

As a high school student he was not interested in sports, the preoccupation of most of the students. "I had a big struggle in high school," he remembered, "because the overarching thing there was basketball, not scholastic achievement. I just didn't have the physical coordination to play sports. My eyesight was bad (I wore glasses). It was just hopeless. I was more interested in the scholastic aspects of school life."[2]

If sports were not attractive, other aspects of school life were. He was active in various areas, for one or more years, including serving as class president and on student council and yearbook staff, and participating in mixed chorus, men's glee club, band, clarinet quartet, and class plays.[3]

David was clearly an excellent student. By March of his freshman year in high school he had completed the work of the algebra book and was beginning to study second-year algebra. While still in high school he was studying college algebra on his own. His mother once commented that David sometimes would rather work on algebra than eat. Throughout his high school years, he earned As, which meant that each year he was on the honor roll. At graduation he was the class valedictorian.

He retained good memories of his high school experience. Years later, in writing to a class reunion that he could not attend, he commented: "I have always been grateful for my rearing and education in the Hamlin community.... I once told Mrs. Vonderschmidt that her typing classes have been extremely helpful. At that time I had no inkling that typing would be so necessary in my medical practice."[4]

Throughout his high school years, he also retained his early interest in talking with people and learning from them. His brother Les tells of a trip that the family took to

California to visit relatives when David was a young teenager. "We became delayed somewhere in the desert in the southwest by a train that was blocking the road. There was a long line of cars backed up on both sides of the track and it appeared that it would be some time before the train moved on. So my brother began to walk through the line of cars, chatting with the waiting people."[5] This interest in conversing with people included speaking with the local railroad section crew who commonly used words never heard in the Byer household.

Spiritual Development

During these years, David was also maturing spiritually. He owed much of his spiritual growth to his parents who were devout Christians. Janet describes the nature of this part of the Byer family life: "We always attended church twice on Sunday plus mid-week prayer meeting. Then we had revival meetings periodically to which we went every night without fail. Our parents instilled in us strong morals and Christian character, accompanied by the necessary discipline when needed. We ate meals together and had daily Bible reading and prayer. Our parents had a strong interest in missions. Many times we hosted visiting missionaries in our home. We visited the Navajo Mission [in New Mexico]."

The Pleasant Hill congregation conveyed the same atmosphere of piety and of obedience to conscience and the Bible. By this time the congregation was small; many of its members, as already noted, had moved from the area. But the remaining members formed a tightly-knit spiritual group. Many of the adults still wore the traditional plain, uniform dress of the denomination, but they did not force this clothing style on the young members.

A reporter for the *St. Joseph Gazette* nicely caught the nature of the congregation in David's youth. After observing that the members were conservative in their dress and observant of the precepts laid down by the apostle Paul, she wrote: "These are a gracious, gentle, kindly people with a strong and courageous character. Their fine, well-kept homes (though simple in lifestyle like their church building) show the result of industry and faith."[6]

David claimed "many fond memories of growing up in the Pleasant Hill congregation.... Everyone there seemed to take a personal interest in me. When I came home from college they would all ask what I was studying.... But how could I explain college and university terms and technology to these farming people?"

At one time, David was virtually the only young person in the congregation, but he was faithful in attending services and in the responsibilities given to him. At a young age he was given charge of the Sunday school offering. Later he held the offices of secretary, treasurer and vice president of Christ's Crusaders, as the youth group was called, although it was comprised mainly and necessarily of congregational members beyond the age of youth.[7] These offices helped to give him a sense of belonging to the congregation.

He did not claim a crisis conversion experience, which was historically normal for Brethren in Christ. Primarily his parents and the congregation nurtured him in the faith. When he was fourteen years of age, he was baptized in the Hamlin Baptist Church baptistry because the area had no open body of water in which Brethren in Christ customarily baptized, and the congregation no longer baptized in a watering trough for horses. At the baptism service were the Kansas bishop and his wife, Ray and Ruth Witter. As was customary, David gave his testimony of faith in Christ before being baptized. After the baptism the congregation sang "Trust and Obey." "I can still hear Aunt Ruth [Witter] singing that song," he fondly remembered.

One of the highlights of the church calendar year for David was the annual love feast. On those occasions members of the small, isolated congregation would be joined by Brethren in Christ from the Abilene area— Lowell and Dorcas Hoover, Mahlon and Irene Engle, and Ray and Ruth Witter among them. Love feasts gave David a sense of belonging to the larger body of Brethren in Christ beyond the small group at Pleasant Hill.

Another highlight for David and the congregation was visits of missionaries, as well as other Brethren in Christ on their way to or from California. In the late 1950s one of these visitors in the Byer home and the congregation was Dr. Alvan Thuma, who established the denominational hospitals at Mtshabezi and Macha missions in Africa. Dr. Thuma "rigged up a car battery with a ten- or twelve-volt light on it so he could see to operate. That really piqued my interest." Dr. Thuma's stories were influential in David's decision to become a medical doctor.

In an article in the *Evangelical Visitor* in 1982, David told of the "interesting variety" of other Brethren in Christ in the Byer home. "How can a boy soon forget the evangelist who signed the guest book [with] Matthew 6:33 ["But seek ye first the kingdom of God…"], because he was more interested that we remember that text than we remember his name? Another guest was the one who wrote, 'Fixed David's toys.'"[8]

Still another highlight of the year for David was the annual youth camp held in Kansas for Brethren in Christ living in that and surrounding states. Largely alone as a youth in the Pleasant Hill congregation, David came into contact with other denominational youth at these conferences. The fellowship with these young people, the worship experiences, and the teaching of such church leaders as Owen Alderfer all impressed him and enriched his life.[9]

This chapter may fittingly end with David's reflection on the influences on his life—from ancestors, family, and church. "Numerous family influences come into play. Piety, the importance of church family, and the view that our citizenship is in our Lord's heavenly kingdom come to mind. The folly of trusting in the promises of earthly rulers is illustrated repeatedly. I cringe at the current expression, 'Take back our country.' I don't know what that means. If it is the call to revert to a time when slavery was practiced, tarring and feathering of perceived enemies [as in the Revolutionary War] and dueling was an acceptable form of conflict resolution, I want nothing to do with it. Instead I claim Hebrews 13:14, 'For here we have no lasting city, but we seek a city that is to come.'"

3

Childhood and Youth: Jeannie

Home Life

Jeannie and her siblings, as noted, grew to adulthood in Africa as children of missionaries. Their parents instilled in them that they were a part of their missionary work, a concept that Jeannie easily and fully accepted.[1]

As Jeannie grew older she became increasingly involved in the life of the mission and her family. She assisted her mother in the clinic in the treatment of patients' eyes for trachoma.[2] Her mother taught her how to sew (a necessity in an area where there were no stores). One summer Jeannie made forty-two simple dresses for local school girls: colored stitching around the neck indicated which grade a girl was in. Another summer she taught a local Sudanese girl how to read. "It was very exciting," Jeannie recalls, "when it dawned on her how reading works."

The children got up early and joined their parents in Bible study and prayer.[3] During the day they were given chores, which were expected to be done with little complaint, even if, as her brother David explains, it was separating seeds from the kopok, which they all hated to do. He remembers sitting with his siblings before mountains of green beans and snapping them for canning.

Their mother made such chores bearable by often turning them into games or story telling. "Each of us got ten minutes or so before the next one took up the story before we stopped. Sometimes the story went on for a couple of days."

All was not work. The siblings played with Sudanese children. They waterskied on the nearby Akobo River. This took skill because crocodiles lived in the water. "Don't fall in! You'll be eaten by crocodiles," they would shout at each other. They often went boating in dug-out canoes. Riding bicycles, climbing trees, and building houses out of bricks were also part of their childhood.

Animals abounded; some were dangerous. One day Jeannie saw a thirsty-looking cat under a tree. When she took it a bowl of milk, the cat bit one of Jeannie's arms and would not release its grip. The animal was rabid, which meant that for twenty-one days Jeannie had to receive rabies shots. A Nuer woman also had been bitten by a rabid animal; each morning little Jeannie and the Sudanese woman walked together to the clinic for their shots.

Humor and pranks were characteristic of this family, surely a saving grace for life in Sudan. David tells of the time the family attended a conference when Jeannie was approximately ten and he was five. "Both of us wanted roller skates but Mom and Dad would not buy them for us. So while our parents were at a meeting during the conference, Jeannie and I gathered thistles and stuffed them into my Dad's pillow.... It was Jeannie's idea, of course."

David relates another story of a time when their dog Kinky had many ticks. "We had beans for lunch. Some of the green beans were over-mature, with large grey beans inside. Jeannie pretended to take a tick from the dog who was sniffing around the table. Then she loudly exclaimed,

'Oh, look at this big tick I found on Kinky.' She held up the grey bean, popped it into her mouth, and bit down on it." When her father was about to discipline her for her action, she exclaimed, "It's only a bean!"

Jeannie and her mother once took a trip to visit some other missionaries. Again, her brother tells the story: "There was a spirit of humor between my mom and the pilot [of the airplane]. When they arrived at their destination, he offered them a drink. It was strong salt water. The pilot apologized and brought another glass of water. It too was salt water. Sometime later Mom and Jeannie entered his room. They found his clothes lying on the bed which they quickly sewed to the sheets. As they were flying home my Mom and Jeannie poured perfume into his flight bag. Back came the pilot's voice, 'Truce, truce!'"

The family found humor in other situations. One of Jeannie's favorite stories is the fate of a piece of her mother's clothing. "Local people wore very little clothing in that tropical area but western clothing was highly prized. One day Mom threw away some of her old underwear. Imagine her horror when, arriving at church the next Sunday, she saw one of the men enter the church wearing her underpants and no other clothing. He had split the crotch, pulled it over his head, and was wearing it as a shirt, with one arm through each leg hole. After that she always cut that kind of clothing into little pieces before throwing it away."

Even as a child, Jeannie showed the concerns and skills of a caregiver, especially to her two younger siblings, Jack and David. David says that when Jeannie was around seven and he a year and a half, a group was on the river in the mission's thirty-foot launch. David was playing with two cans of water when he suddenly fell into the river. Only

Jeannie saw him fall. She jumped into the water, undaunted by the thought of crocodiles, and pulled him to safety. "When Jeannie was around," David says, "I felt that all was right with the world. She had a warm and secure atmosphere about her."

At a young age, Jeannie made her own clothes and did some of the cooking for the family. On David's seventh birthday, she planned and carried out the birthday party for him.

Jeannie grew up in a context different from most Christian children. Her brother writes: "She was surrounded by a number of Godly people—people who had given their lives for the gospel and for the benefit of a people far from their own homes. It was considered the normal way to spend one's life. She was surrounded by medical people and those who needed medical aid. She also grew up where political instability was a way of life. There was the day when my mom and dad said to us, 'If you are on the river side of the house today, crawl in front of the windows. Don't expose yourself to gunfire. There is likely to be shooting on that side of the house today.'"

School

Jeannie's mother home-schooled her to the end of grade three. Then came boarding school. Because further education was unavailable in that part of Sudan, she and her brothers finished their grade and high school education in Egypt. This meant traveling across much of Africa with one parent shepherding them and other children.

Again, in these travels, Jeannie became a caregiver. She was one of the older students who became a guardian of younger children as they journeyed to their destination in Egypt. Jeannie and her traveling companions became intrepid travelers. At train stations they would be assailed by vendors of goods and souvenirs who saw these Westerners as likely targets for their goods. The children would tell them that they had no money to purchase items. After insisting but without success, the vendors would sputter and swear in anger.

The Schutz school which Jeannie attended was located in Assiout and taught an American curriculum. Most of the teachers were from the West. Jeannie remembers a Miss Duff and a Miss Anderson. Both were nice to the children; the former taught handwriting and read books to the children. Paul McClanahan told exciting stories about desert adventures he had taken while he was a boy. He would stop at an exciting part in the story, to resume it the next week, despite the pleas of the children to finish it at once. In contrast to these teachers was the housemother who would hit the children with a broomstick when they did something she didn't like.

But most of Jeannie's experiences at the school were positive. She liked the food, including the date jam with whipped cream inside *aish belady* (whole grain pita bread), and *kenafa*, which was like shredded wheat wrapped around walnuts and drenched in honey. With their allowances, children could buy sugar cane, Turkish delight, and *mortadella* to make salami sandwiches.

The school's geographic setting provided excellent opportunities to explore famous places and to meet Egyptian people. On one occasion, students took a four-day trip into the desert on camels. They rode on the Nile River in *felluccas* (cargo sailboats). Sometimes students visited wealthy Egyptian families. At other times Jeannie spent the weekend in the home of a classmate whose parents lived in town. One Christmas she was in the home of the Paul and

Mary Martha Jamison family. He was a medical missionary, and both were excellent musicians. She played the piano and had a lovely voice; he played a musical saw. The entire family loved music, so there was much singing over the holiday. (Paul and Mary Martha later in life resided in Messiah Village and attended the Grantham Brethren in Christ Church.)

During the years of boarding school, Jeannie was with her parents only in the summer. Until air service became available, travel was by boat and train, which took two weeks to reach Egypt. When travel by air became possible, Jeannie once had the responsibility of carrying a large box of ninety fertilized Rhode Island Red eggs to her father for his work of improving the quality of chickens (thirty-five of the eggs hatched).

The Schutz school eventually moved to Alexandria. Here, too, most of the students were Westerners. But a more cosmopolitan atmosphere now characterized the school. In large part, this feature was owing to the World Health Organization whose headquarters were in the city. Thus children from India, the Philippines, China, Denmark, Germany, and Liberia were Jeannie's schoolmates.

Here too were good teachers, most of them Westerners. Jeannie claims that John Small "taught the only math that I really understood." John and Martha Sisley were an elderly couple. He taught biology. When he gave a test and all students incorrectly answered a question, he would write B. H. (big hearted) and give credit for the incorrect answer. His wife was a "sweet little lady" who taught Latin and English. She was obviously a good teacher: papers for which Jeannie earned a B at Schutz earned her an A when reworked as college papers.

Relocating the school gave new opportunities for travel and cultural enrichment. Jeannie and fellow students visited King Farouk's palace, attended a performance by the Leningrad Ballet, and sometimes went with non-boarding students to their homes and the Sporting Club. Some of these activities came as rewards for well-kept rooms.

In 1956, while Jeannie was in school in Alexandria, the American Embassy warned the school to evacuate because war was coming. The school temporarily closed. Those students whose parents lived in Egypt were evacuated by the American Sixth Fleet to Naples, Italy; students from Sudan were sent to their parents. As Jeannie and other students traveled south, French and English planes bombed each of the airports at Alexandria, Cairo, and Luxor before the children were able to take flight from them. Their travel by train ended when the tracks were bombed. In detouring the tracks by car, a tire blew out; the passengers thought they had been hit by a bomb. From Luxor, a paddlewheel boat and a slow train took Jeannie and the other students to Khartoum in Sudan. What greater excitement could a child ask for?

Becoming a Christian

During these years, Jeannie became a Christian. One of the influences leading her to this decision was the pilot of the airplane who flew her on the first leg of the trip to Egypt. Gordon Marshal exhibited the best in Christianity. She writes: "I decided I wanted Christ as my Lord after watching his patience and kindness. He usually had very limited space in his tiny plane, and a tight schedule to get back to base before dark. People would show up late and with twice as much stuff and more passengers than he could carry, but he wouldn't get angry. He would kindly explain what he could carry, and would revise his schedule. As he took us on the first day of our trip, sometimes he would do a few acrobatic moves or swoop down to see herds of elephants, both to take our minds off of leaving home."

Reading C. S. Lewis's *Screwtape Letters* in Sunday school was another influence in making her decision to become a Christian. "Screwtape was telling Wormwood that they could capture the man by getting him complacent. He didn't need to be blatantly sinning, he just needed to think he was OK while not doing God's will.... I hadn't realized that I was guilty of the sin of omission. I decided to try to do wholeheartedly all of God's will."

Cultural Experiences in the United States

While in Sudan and later in Ethiopia, the family had two furloughs in the United States. Not surprisingly, Jeannie experienced some culture shock. During the first furlough the family lived in College Station, Texas, while her father studied at Texas A&M University. On one occasion her parents spoke to a congregation comprised of wealthy people. After the service they greeted the people— of course, with a smile. One woman said to Jeannie's mother, "Everything you give to them takes away from us." Another woman told her, "You're doing it wrong. Haven't you heard about the world's overpopulation? If you give medical aid to those people, they will continue to live and make more children and the world will be overpopulated." "We were shocked," Jeannie writes. "We believed we were helping God's people."

In Texas, the family quickly gained a reputation for liking African-Americans. Jeannie could not understand the negative reaction to her playing with black children. In

Africa she had played with black children all the time, and she had a black doll. "Our response to those who criticized us," Jeannie says, "was that Africans treat us a lot better than you do." Obviously these Texans had never interacted personally with another race.

In College Station the family first attended a Presbyterian church. Soon they attended a Methodist church because they thought that the Presbyterian church did not follow biblical teaching. One Sunday, at the invitation of the Presbyterian congregation, an African-American minister preached. The Jordans were asked to invite the black minister to their home for lunch: no one in the Presbyterian congregation wanted to eat with him. "Sure, of course," the Jordans replied. Jeannie concludes the story by saying, "We had the best afternoon with that man. He was a marvelous minister."

Another kind of culture shock awaited the children on the second furlough, just after the Suez war experience. This one they spent in Pittsburgh, Pennsylvania, with their Aunt Edith who lived next door to where their mother had grown up. On the first day in school, the practice siren sounded. "Jack and I dived under our desks," Jeannie recalls. 'What are you doing there?' the teacher asked. 'It's a siren,' we said. 'We are supposed to get under something heavy in case there is a bomb!' They all laughed, but we would not come out until they got our mother on the phone and she told us it was OK."

We may read Jeannie's early experiences as influencing and characterizing her adult life. Her medical work, love of travel, association with people of different races and nationalities, interest in missions, caring attitude, self-reliance, ability to make things happen—all of these, and more, were surely all shaped by her childhood and youth.

4

Medical Training, Courtship and Marriage

Decisions on Medical Careers

At first thought, associating medicine with marriage may seem somewhat strange. But as this chapter shows, the two are part of the whole. Both David and Jeannie decided on a medical career, and they began their courtship during their studies in this field.

Various factors led David into medicine. He had severe allergies caused by grain, which he knew would prevent him from being a lifelong Kansas farmer. Also he thrived on math and science, especially chemistry and biology, subjects that seemed a natural entrance into the medical profession. As noted, his attendance at the two summer science camps sponsored by the University of Kansas served to reinforce his interest in these subjects. And it may be assumed that his inquisitive mind and his love of research and doing experiments would be well fulfilled in a medical career. Undoubtedly his father's early failed hopes to be a medical missionary also played on David's thinking.

But perhaps the greatest influence leading him to medicine was the example of medical doctors. Among them was Ray Meidinger, the family doctor in Hiawatha (a nearby town). Also, as noted, Dr. Alvan Thuma, while visiting in the Byer home and the Pleasant Hill congregation, sparked David's interest in medical missionary work. Still another doctor from whom David drew inspiration was Alvin Heise, who was with the Navajo Mission hospital when David was at the Mission with a work team from the Abilene church.

But where would he obtain his education? Brethren in Christ young people usually first considered one of the denomination's two colleges—Messiah College in Pennsylvania and Upland College in California. David decided to attend the latter. Some of his relatives lived in the Upland area, including his Byer grandmother, Tissot grandparents, aunts and a great aunt. By going to Upland College he would be following where most Kansas Brethren in Christ young people went. And there he was more likely than at Messiah College to obtain employment to help with college expenses (a prospect that attracted students from as far away as provinces in Canada).

So to Upland College he went. Of the courses he took during his one year there, he especially liked the classes taught by science professor Anna Leatherman. "Her interests," David says, "very much matched mine."

He earned some income by working for his uncle Homer Warner, who had a dead animal business. David would accompany his uncle to dairy farms to collect carcasses, which were then sent to a tannery. He admits that "it was not the most pleasant job, but it paid me and helped with my expenses."

At the end of the year, however, David returned to Kansas to become a student at the University of Kansas. Pursuing a degree there would be less financially burdensome for his parents. Also, the likelihood of obtaining entrance into medical school would be greater at the Kansas university than if he applied from a still unaccredited small college.

At the University of Kansas, David majored in chemistry. After graduating from the undergraduate program in 1963, he entered the university's medical school, from which he graduated in 1967.

In 1961 Jeannie left Africa for the United States to obtain a degree in nursing. She made the trip alone, much to the amazement of her grandfather, but to Jeannie this was a "breeze" considering her experiences of traveling in Africa.

Like David she had decided to study in a medical area. Her choice, in part, was based on her experience of working with her mother in the clinic in Africa, and, in part, because she was not attracted to what she understood to be alternatives open to her—being a secretary or a teacher.

After spending some time with relatives in Pittsburgh, Pennsylvania, and eastern Illinois, Jeannie traveled to Kansas to enter Sterling College, a Presbyterian school. Here she had as schoolmates some international students and children of missionaries, who, because of backgrounds similar to her own, helped to ease her into college life and make it more interesting. One of her roommates lived only fifty miles from the college and went home on weekends. Still, the student cried nightly from loneliness. This puzzled Jeannie: "I had been away from home throughout the whole school year since I was eight years old. I didn't understand what the problem was."

Her time at Sterling College was made all the more pleasant by being "adopted" by John and Lois Colburn in whose home she spent some weekends, holidays, and vacations. Their daughter Phyllis Tucker has written the following account of the warm relationship between

Jeannie and the Colburn family: "A mutual friend of my parents and Jeannie's parents, Aleta Matthews, knew that Jeannie would need a 'home away from home.' She put our families in touch with each other and Jeannie lived with us during vacations from Sterling College. And I got a sister [Jeannie says the same of Phyllis].

"Even though she was a college student and I was in elementary school, Jeannie had unlimited patience, sharing a room with me, helping me wash dishes while teaching me 'Tiki Tiki Tambo,' making a whole new wardrobe of tiny clothes for my Barbie doll, and always treating me as a friend, not as a little kid.

"One of her college friends married a young man from our church, and Jeannie and I were asked to help with the reception. I'd had minor surgery on a foot and my dress shoes wouldn't fit over the bandage, so Jeannie and I took turns wearing her shoes when we picked up dirty dishes from guests. Now that's true sisterly love—she shared her shoes. Best of all she asked me to be a junior bridesmaid at her wedding.

"Jeannie and David often went out of their way on trips to come to my parents' house or my house [after my marriage]. Recently I read my grandmother's diary and discovered that they also stopped often to see my grandparents. Jeannie makes family her priority, and she considers many nonrelatives as part of her family. I am thankful that Jeannie adopted me as her sister. She has made my world much larger."[1]

The relationship between Jeannie and Phyllis—and the family—may be illustrated by the love letters escapade. The two girls found boxes of love letters written by Phyllis's parents. They selected several letters and mailed them back to the elder Colburns from various locations in the surrounding area.

At the end of her second year at Sterling College, Jeannie transferred to the University of Kansas to continue studies towards a nursing degree. During summers she worked as a nurse's aide at the fourteen-bed hospital in Jetmore, Kansas. Her work load was strenuous—three sixteen-hour shifts each week. Here she shared a room with another former Sterling student. "We joked," she recalls, "that we never had to make the bed because we took turns being in it."

Shortly before graduating with her nursing degree, Jeannie decided to buy a car. Her description of how she financed her purchase illustrates her character: "My parents, who had promised to buy my first car, were living in a very remote area in Ethiopia and I had no way of contacting them for money. However, I was confident that they would send me the money when they heard about my need. So I went to a bank for a loan. The questions I was asked to answer on a form made me feel helpless. 'How many months out of the last two years have you been unemployed?' I answered, 'Twenty-four.' 'How long do you plan to stay in your present home?' I wrote, 'Three weeks.' 'Are you currently employed?' I answered, 'No.' 'What is your current salary per month?' My response was '0.'

"As the man went into a back room, my hopes fell. When he came out, he was laughing. He said, 'You must be honest. Nobody would fill out a form like you did unless they were honest.' He gave me the loan and I bought a brand new Bahama blue Volkswagen for $1,779. My parents sent the money and I repaid the loan in two weeks."

Courtship

Meanwhile, David and Jeannie had fallen in love. However, the story is not as simple as that statement suggests because David had earlier been attracted to a young woman in Kansas City. In fact, the two had become engaged. The fiancée's mother was delighted: her daughter would be marrying a doctor and living in Kansas City, and they would all be well cared for.

However, although engaged, David had doubts about the marriage. The last thing he wanted to do was to practice medicine in Kansas City. Also, his fiancée carried around a little dog, something that David's mother found objectionable.

Then David met Jeannie while both were students at the university. The university's cafeteria offered meals at half price if bought after 11 p.m. Coming from frugal families, such dining appealed to both of them. In this delightful setting, in the context of inexpensive food, the two came to know each other.

"I was just fascinated by this young woman," David said. So they began to meet in more places than the university cafeteria. They sometimes ate in an inexpensive Mexican restaurant near the university. When Paul Brandt, the noted leprosy surgeon from India, lectured at the university, Jeannie skipped a class to accompany David to the lecture.

When David and Jeannie began to date, she at first delayed telling her mother of her developing romantic interest. "If I wrote to my mother that I went on a date," she explains, "she would write back to tell me not to get married until I was finished school. I would tell her that it was just a date. Then she would write back saying, 'Well, I don't want you to be an old-age single missionary.'"

A significant point in their relationship came on a trip to David's home in Brown County. He had planned to take his fiancée with him, but she was unable to accompany him. With considerable apprehension, David invited Jeannie to take his fiancée's place. She accepted.

Their time in Brown County introduced Jeannie to the Brethren in Christ at Pleasant Hill. "I didn't understand," she recalled, "what they meant when they said, 'Who were you?' My response was, 'I've always been me.' When David explained that they wanted to know my genealogy, I told them that my father was Charles Jordan, but they were puzzled because they didn't know the Jordans. Clearly I was an outsider. But I'm glad they accepted me."

The rest of Jeannie's visit in Brown County went well. She writes, "It was so great to be on the Byer farm. I liked David's siblings, Janet and Les. Janet and I enjoyed grooming the dog. Everett and Adela were a lot like my parents, and I really enjoyed being in their home." Shortly before her marriage she wrote to her future in-laws saying that she will "enjoy being part of your family."

In Jeannie, David was certain that he had found the right person to be his wife. Following time together in New Mexico, he wrote about her to his parents in a letter dated September 6, 1965. "The wheels of the El Cap sing a different song than those of the Chief [names of trains]. The Chief says, 'I'm taking you to Jeannie. I'm taking you to Jeannie.' The wheels of the El Cap sing, 'Back to work. Back to work.'"

"We sure had a good time together out in New Mexico. I wouldn't trade it for anything. You know, we didn't even quarrel once—in fact we never have, and she is much more stubborn about some things than some other girls I've gone with. The big difference is that she always has a good reason behind her thinking—better than 'just because.'

"Dr. Gordon [for whom she worked] says she is the most level-headed nurse he has. How I ever latched on to someone as good as her I'll never know. She sure can make the Gordon kids behave. They listen to her and she doesn't allow any horseplay.... I'm of the opinion that she is going to make a good wife."

The result of this growing interest in each other led David to break his engagement and to propose marriage to Jeannie. He made his proposal in California. The two had traveled by airplane to that state to visit his Tissot grandparents and other relatives. "I was a little surprised," Jeannie remembers, "at how many Byer and Tissot relatives there were. I got a lot more, "Who were you?'"

While in California, David and Jeannie went for a drive up Mount Baldy north of Upland, a popular activity (including for Upland College students). There on the slopes of the mountain on Christmas Eve 1965, David asked Jeannie to be his wife. She accepted his proposal: "He was such a nice man."

Much of their courtship was long-distance. After graduation, Jeannie worked as a nurse with Dr. Robert Gordon, whom she knew in Africa, at the Mora Valley Medical Unit in New Mexico, sponsored by Presbyterians. Here her work frequently involved the results of over-consumption of alcoholic beverages, especially beer. (The town, with a population of 400 residents, had eighteen bars.) One man came to the clinic with three leg fractures. He explained, "I was just sitting on the bar stool and my leg swelled up." A previous doctor at the clinic said she planned to write a book entitled *Just Two Beers* because that was a common explanation of how injuries occurred.

On a few occasions David and Jeannie managed to come together. They would meet at a place somewhere between their two locations, sometimes at the Colburns' residence. On one occasion after being together at the Colburns, they drove to Dodge City where David traveled back to Kansas City by train. After the train had left the station, David realized, too late, that he still had the keys to the car. Because this action occurred more than once, Jeannie obtained two sets of keys.

The Wedding

Prior to the wedding, Jeannie drove her trusty Volkswagen back to Kansas with her possessions on board. Before reaching the Byers' residence, the engine ran out of oil. Jeannie coasted off the interstate to a nearby garage where she called David and his father. They drove to meet her. The car's engine needed replacing, but surely no one took that as a bad omen for the upcoming wedding and marriage.

David and Jeannie married on December 23, 1966, virtually a year after their engagement. In the previous year, her parents had brought Ethiopian fabric for her wedding dress and for the bridesmaids' dresses. When making her dress, Jeannie cut and sewed the materials very carefully because there was no extra fabric in case she made a mistake.

Their wedding was the first in the new Presbyterian church in Jetmore, Kansas. The church's pastor, Rev. James Rhaesa, conducted the ceremony. David's best man, his roommate at the university, was so nervous that Hiram, the patriarch of the Colburn family, gave him some brandy to calm him.

The wedding was relatively simple, in keeping with the couple's lifestyle. Reporting on the wedding to family members, David's mother wrote, "The wedding was the kind of wedding I like—simple and meaningful."[2] Before the wedding the couple had consulted with Dorothy (Witter) Schrag, Bishop Witter's daughter, on suggestions for music. The Byers recall that one song was "Praise the Lord, King of Creation."

The couple had planned for a honeymoon that would take them to a ranch at the bottom of the Grand Canyon. But before leaving they received a message saying that the trail to the ranch was flooded. They could not much regret this news because they did not have enough money for such a trip. Instead they honeymooned in Colorado. Adela reported that they spent the first two nights in a motel at $5.00 a night so they could afford to spend the rest of the time at Deer Valley Ranch, whose owner's daughter had attended Sterling College with Jeannie.

5

Medical Careers

Continued Medical Training

Following their honeymoon in Colorado, David and Jeannie returned to Kansas. Jeannie worked as a nurse in the Gardner, Kansas, Community Hospital, approximately thirty-two miles southwest of Kansas City. While listed as a part-time nurse, in effect she was actually more than full-time; she had only three days off from her work during the three months she was employed there.

After a month, David joined her to do his rural Kansas preceptorship. The couple lived in a room in the basement of the hospital. Their bed was two hospital beds tied together by wire coat hangers. The room was below the delivery room, which allowed David to dash up the spiral staircase when called to a delivery.

Because Jeannie worked during the day, including Sunday, they enjoyed attending the evening services of the Hillcrest Covenant Church in Prairie Village. Thus when they later became members of the Salem Road Covenant Church in Rochester, Minnesota, they already were acquainted with the Covenant denomination.

While at Gardner, both David and Jeannie obtained grants to do medical work in Ethiopia (see the following chapter for their work there). Following three months in that country they returned to Kansas to attend David's graduation from medical school and to take a three-week camping trip to California. This adventure included camping near a big snowbank at Donner Pass and on Mount Tamalpais near San Francisco. At another time a huge downpour of rain thoroughly soaked the tent and its occupants. Travel would become a characteristic of the couple and later their family.

After this trip the couple settled in Wichita, Kansas, where David did his internship at Wesley Medical Center, and where Jeannie found nursing work at Wichita Clinic. Each received a paycheck on alternate weeks, thus providing a steady income; together they lived more comfortably than one. From this comfortable income, they set aside one-half to finance later travel to Africa. They obviously had sufficient income for Jeannie to take flying lessons and obtain her private pilot's license.

She received a compliment, of sorts, one day on going to the hospital to meet David for dinner at the hospital cafeteria. A security guard stopped her, saying that no one under fourteen was allowed to enter. The guard relented when she showed him her wedding ring and told him that she was Dr. Byer's wife.

The Mayo Clinic

At the end of David's internship, he and Jeannie flew to Zambia for a term of medical service, but before leaving David obtained an interview at the Mayo Clinic in Rochester, Minnesota, where he hoped to be accepted for a residency in anesthesiology.

His decision to follow this medical specialty was owing to various factors. At the time, anesthesiologists were in demand across the country, including at Mayo Clinic.

Moreover, his inclination in this direction was sharpened by his association with two anesthesiologists at the Wesley Medical Center, both trained at Mayo Clinic.

David explained an element in his decision: "For some reason the idea of general practice never came under direct consideration. I'm not sure I can say that I rejected the idea of general practice. Rather, anesthesiology took precedence. The way was open [for me to enter this field]. Frankly, I felt more comfortable confining my interests to a narrow segment of medicine than in doing general practice."

He considered applying for a residency position in several places across the country—Kansas City, Pittsburgh, Los Angeles, San Francisco, among others. Then why did he choose Mayo Clinic? Obviously it was a very prestigious medical center. But there were other considerations, as he indicates: "We couldn't think of any town the size of Rochester, located in a corn field, that would provide the sort of practice I would enjoy. The idea of living in a large suburban area didn't appeal to us at all. Salary was not a consideration. Organized medicine in those days was especially critical of physicians who worked for a salary, as I would at Mayo Clinic. We disagreed. We knew we would make less at Mayo Clinic, but earning a large amount of money was not nearly as important to us as careful stewardship of the money we earned."

But what hope could he have that he would be accepted at such a place as Mayo Clinic? "It was a long shot," he says, "but I thought I would go for it." The interview resulted in David being accepted into residency. Mayo Clinic agreed that he could begin following his and Jeannie's work in Zambia.

Following service in Zambia (see chapter 7), David and Jeannie settled in Rochester. David began his residency on January 1, 1971, in the midst of a Minnesota blizzard.

David spent his entire professional career at Mayo Clinic, apart from a few years in Africa. At the clinic he served as Assistant Professor of Anesthesiology. When he was on emergency call he provided anesthesia for the various departments and specialists, but he was usually assigned to work with orthopedic and plastic surgeons. He considered orthopedics especially fitting because of the use of regional anesthesia to block pain without patients undergoing general anesthesia. Towards the end of his career at Mayo he became involved with his department in providing post-operative pain relief with peripheral nerve blocks.

He shared also in the development of new techniques. The Division of Radiotherapy was involved in promoting radiation therapy during surgical procedures for certain types of cancer. He was part of the team that helped to develop methods that allowed the anesthetized patient to be left alone during the radiation treatment.

David was one of the first at Mayo Clinic to begin using the fiberoptic bronchoscope, a manipulable and flexible tube through which the upper airway can be visualized. This was helpful in placing an endotracheal tube in patients with deformities of the mouth or neck. In orthopedic surgery, sometimes there were patients with severe cervical spine deformities from rheumatoid arthritis whose backs were inflexible. By using this helpful device, tracheostomy could be avoided. A colleague, Dr. Peter Southorn, recalls that on one occasion, by using this device, David saved the life of a child with a life-threatening airway problem.[1]

For about six years, David was a member of the liver transplanting team. He was the anesthesiologist for Mayo Clinic's first combined heart and liver transplant in 1992.

He also made a significant contribution to patient safety with the anesthesia call-light system. Another colleague, Dr. Steven Rettke, states that this is a "farsighted method of communication within the operating suite and areas of coverage responsibility."[2]

David was held in high regard by his colleagues for his contribution to forward-looking medical techniques and for his exemplary attitude towards patients. Two quotations illustrate the general opinion of staff with whom he worked.

Dr. Rettke writes: "He was a perfectionist for patient confidentiality and an advocate for public safety. He paid meticulous attention to detail, developed confidence, and would answer patients' concerns and questions in a very caring manner.... Dr. Byer displayed a broad range of curiosity and interests in his career. It was said among his colleagues to never underestimate Dr. Byer. He was a keen observer....

"Overall, Dr. Byer could be described as a perceptive, aware, and keen observer.... No task would be too small. Dr. Byer has a quiet and pleasing personality.... For those who know him best, the most lasting impression is his selfless generosity to others, whether through his sharing of knowledge, financial resources, or simple friendship."[3]

Dr. Peter Southorn comments: "As long as I have known David, and this goes back to our medical residency days together, he has always been a quiet, reserved and outstanding human being, solid as a rock, and completely unflappable. His ability to safely care for and manage the most difficult and trying medical problems became evident early in his career. This has not always been easy, given the complexity of many Mayo Clinic patients' medical problems and the fact that in the operating room one has to work with people who have [other tasks]. This ability to never lose control of the safe care of patients has given David the reputation of being a clinical anesthesiologist *par excellence*, both within the institution and the broader anesthetic community outside."[4]

As Dr. Southorn's last sentence indicates, David was active in the medical world beyond his work at Mayo Clinic. His vita shows that he attended numerous conferences and workshops in Minnesota, Washington, D. C., and elsewhere in the United States, and similar meetings in other countries—for a total of seventy-one. According to his impressive twenty-five-page vita, he presented papers in fourteen countries, including the Netherlands, Spain, South Africa, Turkey, Brazil, the United Kingdom, India, Ghana, and Germany (several times each in Germany and the United Kingdom). He taught 107 courses both within and outside Mayo Clinic, many of them case studies.

Additionally, he was an active member of state and national medical organizations, and held official positions in ten of them. Undoubtedly the most noteworthy of these positions was with the Minnesota Society of Anesthesiology. There he rose from membership rank to be treasurer, then secretary, vice president, and editor. He was also a member of the Board of Directors of the American Society of Anesthesiologists, District 15, in which his leadership, according to Dr. Rettke, "sustained the membership within the Society and forwarded the profession of anesthesiology."[5]

Still another of David's medical activities was as a reviewer for the American Society of Anesthesiologists for the Closed Claims Project relating to medical lawsuits. He volunteered for this position because he wanted to continue to make contributions to the safety of patients. The project was the first of its kind in the United States and generated over 200 articles responding to patient safety.

The nature of this work and why it was important to him are best explained in David's words. "The main purpose of the sub-committee is to aid physicians in improving their clinical practices. Various professional liability insurance companies made their anesthesiology-related claims available to us to examine. I visited insurance company offices in Minneapolis, St. Paul, Harrisburg, Nashville, and Kansas City....

"We prepared a ten-page data collection document. To the best of our abilities we attempted to determine the issues leading to a lawsuit and the disposition of the claim. We were to give an opinion on whether or not the standard of care had been given.

"Main goals of our work were to determine what changes in practice may help prevent complications [thus saving lives] and the filing of a lawsuit. For instance, the administration of a special anesthetic sometimes leads to hypotension. Depending upon how hypotension is treated, blood pressure may be restored. Early detection and treatment is needed. Some medications are much more effective than others. In some instances cardiac arrest and death have happened.

"This is the sort of outcome that understandably may lead to a lawsuit. By conducting claims reviews, the committee could make recommendations in medication and management at a national level in an attempt to improve patient safety."

Clearly, David had a fulfilling medical career at Mayo Clinic. He made significant contributions in the field of anesthesiology, thereby earning the respect and appreciation of colleagues. Towards his patients he could exercise his caring nature, thus earning the gratitude of those whom he served.

6

To Ethiopia

Medical Work at Pokwo

Africa was a significant element in the lives of David and Jeannie. This was not by accident. From their early years, the continent had influenced them. As noted, Jeannie grew to adulthood in two African countries—Sudan and Egypt. Her parents remained in Ethiopia until their evacuation in 1977.

The influence of Africa on David came through the Brethren in Christ Church and its sponsorship of missions in what are now Zambia and Zimbabwe. He knew of the denominational involvement in Africa through various means. As noted, missionaries frequently visited in the Byer home and spoke in the Pleasant Hill church, including Dr. Alvan Thuma who began a hospital at Mtshabezi Mission in Zimbabwe and later at Macha in Zambia (David and Jeannie would serve in both hospitals). His father had hoped to do medical work in Africa, but this hope ended when the family needed him at home following the death of his father. And David would surely have read some of the many stories and reports of missionaries and their work in the pages of the *Evangelical Visitor*, the denominational paper to which most Brethren in Christ of David's parents' age subscribed.

While living and working in Gardner, David and
Jeannie applied for a grant from the pharmaceutical
company Smith, Kline and French to do medical work in
rural Ethiopia. Their choice of location was Pokwo in the
far western part of the country. Here Dr. Dan Reynolds was
stationed; Jeannie knew him from the time that she helped
care for his children. Pokwo was also the place where
Jeannie's parents called for medical advice. David and
Jeannie would be at Pokwo for three months, which would
fulfill requirements for the last three months of David's
medical education.

But would they receive the grant? No response came
from Smith, Kline and French. However, the Byers were
still determined to go, so the couple made reservations.
Only three days before their flight, they received notice that
they had received the grant, which included funds for both
David and Jeannie because she would be working as a
nurse.

Pokwo was a Presbyterian mission station situated
among the Anuak, a Nilotic tribe. There Dr. Dan Reynolds
and Dr. Carroll Lewis, the Byers' mentors, gave them
excellent training in how to do good medical care working
only with essentials.

David and Jeannie visited with her parents at Adura
during their time at Pokwo because the Jordans were not
able to attend their daughter's wedding. These visits were
opportunities to be with their now-married daughter and
their new son-in-law. Jeannie's mother taught David how
to do the eyelid surgery that she herself had done for many
years.

The couple had diversions from their medical work.
Several times David wrote to his parents telling them he
had gone fishing, both at Pokwo and at Adura. One letter

tells of catching a thirty-pound Nile perch. He adds that while fishing, he saw several crocodiles and that a Peace Corps man had recently been eaten by one (hardly reassuring words for parents to read).[1] Two days later he was fishing again, this time with Dr. Loomis of the medical staff. He caught a twenty-pound catfish and a "nice sized tiger fish which has sharp teeth about one inch long…but [they] are not as good eating as Nile perch because they are bonier."[2] In a letter to his sister Janet he wrote about eating spareribs of a wild pig that someone had killed. "They sure are good. Nothing is much better than a Nile perch, however. That meat almost melts in your mouth."[3]

Cultural Observations

This being David's first encounter with an entirely different culture, his letters home frequently made observations about the people and customs of the area. Both David and Jeannie were keen observers of culture, including the African culture both here and later in Zambia and Zimbabwe. David's letters show him to be very interested in and respectful of cultures, and of being descriptive rather than critical.

This attitude may be seen in his correspondence with his parents and sister. In one letter he wrote about the mother of the woman on whom he had done surgery. "[She] asked Jeannie for some IV tubing the other day from which to make a necklace. She was real happy when we gave it to her. She is making a pot for Jean. When Jean was sick this woman was real worried when she didn't see 'Jinni,' and asked about her. Of course, I couldn't reply [in her language] so I beckoned her to come with me to where Jean was and when she saw Jean she got all excited and blessed her by spitting on her [Jeannie's] hands."[4] This is one of many stories David shared to illustrate the friendliness and kindness of Africans.

In the same letter to Janet, he described other cultural experiences. "A nearby village," he wrote, "is having a dance and we can hear their drums and chanting.... It sounds just like you see on TV and I almost expect them to come and get us to put in their pot any moment." In the letter he told of being served African food. "One of the native guys serves dinner and since I don't know their language I would say 'yum yum' when something tasted good. Came to find out that this word was used by them in reference to cannibals!!"

Also in this letter he described the nature of a church service he had attended. "They use drums in the church services and sing chants which translate into something about how Jesus came to earth and was good and died and we should follow him. Last Sunday the school boys present-ed a skit about the prodigal son. It was really good. They were at their best when the [prodigal son] was in a far coun-try enjoying himself dancing. They just didn't seem to quit dancing."[5] Surely the scene was interesting to the writer who had grown up in a denomination which, in his youth, disapproved of dancing.

In one of his letters to his parents, David again wrote about drums, this time with an apparent "tongue in cheek." "After listening to the drums last night I decided to make a tape this p.m. which can be played as a special number at church when we get back."[6] His comments on music show his preference for Western-oriented styles. He tells his parents that he has been "listening to some real dippy Arabic music...the kind Jeannie heard all the time in Alexandria. It is a real whiny high pitched wailing five-note scale. Must say I prefer Mormon Tabernacle Choir or New York Philharmonic."[7]

His cultural experiences included buying an Ethiopian pipe. He wrote to his parents: "Today bought a real nice 28" pipe for $4 (Et) = $1.60 U.S., from the old Nuer lady. We would like to take it to the United States with us. It is nice and smelly. Everybody laughed at me as I carried it to the house. Now if we could just get hold of some spears."[8]

Connecting with Westerners

The Byers made several significant contacts while in Africa. At the end of their service they visited Kenya and Mike Brown who was teaching English at Eumusere Secondary School, a small Church of God (Anderson) boys school, working under the Mennonite Central Committee's Teachers Abroad Program (TAP). Mike has written appreciatively of the many miles that the Byers took in a hair-raising ride across the mountains to visit him. He notes that David and he had been students together at Upland College. In the early 1900s both grandfathers—Arthur Tissot and Alfred Brown—had farmed near each other on the east side of Chino. David's mother and Mike's father had both attended the same school. Because Mike's father had poor eyesight, David's mother served as one of his textbook readers. Mike writes that his father was grateful to the end of his life for that service.[9]

This trip illustrates David and Jeannie's interest in a wide variety of people and their willingness to go out of their way—physically and metaphorically—to help and encourage them.

Another significant contact was with Arlene Schuiteman, a nurse supported by the Reformed Church of America. She had helped to open what was called a dresser school in the city of Mettu, where she taught wound care and other medical skills to health care workers. Some years later, at the encouragement of David and Jeannie, she would serve as nursing instructor at the Brethren in Christ Macha Mission in Zambia.

Not least of their contacts was with Dr. Robert and Winnie Worman, the result of an accidental meeting. On the trip to visit Mike Brown, they encountered the Wormans at the Addis Ababa airport. In Nairobi, Kenya, they unexpectedly met again at a hotel when the Byers were returning from that trip. The two couples had dinner together. "They told us about Macha Hospital in Zambia," the Byers say. "We already knew of this work from the home ministries of Alvan and Ardys Thuma. This meeting played a part in our decision to eventually go to Macha."

7

Medical Service in Zambia

Travel to Africa

On returning to the United States, the Byers became residents of Wichita, Kansas, where, as noted, David did his internship and Jeannie continued to do nursing. At the end of the internship, Africa beckoned again. Africa had never been far from their minds.

Their thinking is caught in a letter from David to his parents. "We have really enjoyed our year in Wichita…. We liked our work, friends, and church fellowship so much. Nevertheless we are glad that the Lord made it possible to serve him in Zambia, and we're eagerly anticipating serving there."[1]

In Zambia, David would be fulfilling his Selective Service obligation. He had obtained a deferment in 1960 because of his medical studies. Now was the time to revisit that obligation, which he would fulfill by working in the Brethren in Christ hospital at Macha.

By registering 1-W he was taking the position of a conscientious objector to war. Given that through their history the Brethren in Christ have been a peace church, such a position on his part is understandable. This was not in Jeannie's tradition, but she was sympathetic to her husband's views on peace.

As noted, after completing his internship in 1967, David visited the Mayo Clinic where he had a successful interview granting him a residency and a postponement of his entry into the program. Following the interview, he flew to Chicago where Jeannie, who had remained in Kansas to pick up his medical license, met him. The couple flew to London and from there to Africa, making several stops on their way to Zambia.

At a Chad airport they encountered extremely hot weather and large, open carts of cattle carcasses, covered with flies, waiting to be loaded on to the plane. Their stop there gave them opportunities to visit several missions. At Bangui, Central African Republic, they expected to be met by the Leland Anderson family who would take them to Zaire, but they did not appear: the Andersons had been given tickets by President Mobuto to fly to the United States for the summer. The Byers went to the United States Embassy where they were directed to the Baptist Mission which had a guest house.

They were graciously received at the Mission, and invited to accompany the director and his wife to the hospital where the wife was scheduled to have a blood test. The Byers saw the four-story hospital building with sewage flowing from the toilets at each end. On entering the lab they were horrified to see the technician grope around in a tub of murky water to find a syringe and needle to draw the blood. David stopped him and recommended that the woman go to another country with better hygiene.

Providence was surely with the Byers in their flight out of the city. The Mission director had gone to the airport to mail letters and there met the pilot who was to fly the Byers to Zaire. But the Byers were at the Mission, not at the airport, thus the pilot began to file his flight plans to return to Zaire. The director informed the pilot that his passengers were at the Mission!

In Zaire the Byers visited missions of the Covenant Church and the Evangelical Free Church. At Karawa, David acted as the anesthesiologist for the operation on the broken arm of a boy who had fallen from a tree. They stayed in Kinshasa before flying to Nairobi, Kenya, where they met the Donavon Nissley family, friends from California. Their last flight took them to Lusaka, Zambia, where they were met by Brethren in Christ missionary Ira (Pete) Stern. Dr. Robert and Winnie Worman, whom the Byers had met in Ethiopia, drove them in a VW Kombi to Macha Mission.

Macha Mission

Macha Mission dates from 1906. Its founders were two women—Frances Davidson and Adda Engle. Davidson was a member of the small handful of Brethren in Christ from the United States who in 1898 began denominational mission work in Africa at Matopo in present-day Zimbabwe. After several years at Matopo, Davidson became convinced that God was calling her to new fields of service. She and Adda Engle traveled by railroad to Livingstone, and from there over many miles by oxen and wagon to Macha.

Under the brilliant mind and unquenchable energy of Frances Davidson, Macha Mission prospered (Adda Engle soon married Myron Taylor and together they established Sikalongo Mission some thirty miles from Macha). The Mission began a school, constructed a church building, opened a clinic (which in 1955 became a hospital under the direction of Dr. Alvan Thuma), and developed a large herd of cattle. In Davidson's years at Macha, the place grew to become one of the most (if not the most) advanced of the denomination's missions in the two Africa countries.[2]

In an undated letter to his parents shortly after their arrival, David described the hospital where he was now engaged: "It has 120 beds, is staffed by two doctors and several nurses, is equipped with x ray, has surgery facilities and a nursing school. A number of outlying clinics are visited from time to time by one of the doctors. The hospital has a chapel. A generator provides a 220-volt current."[3]

The Byers were pleasantly surprised by what they saw. A few months later, David wrote to his parents saying, "The hospital and living quarters are the nicest of any African mission hospital that we have seen." Next month he commented that "things here are not primitive at all compared with Ethiopia, Congo or Chad." Still later he observed that "everyone is always so impressed with the size and neatness and well-equipped nature of our hospital. It was quite a surprise to me too, when I first arrived."[4]

In their first week at Macha, they witnessed what they called two exciting events. One was the death and funeral of Chief Macha. The president of the country, Kenneth Kaunda, attended, as did Elijah Mudenda, the chief's son and the country's Minister of Finance (Mudenda was reared in the Brethren in Christ Church), and a large retinue of ministers and commissioners. (The meal prepared for the guests had to be changed when it was learned at nearly the last minute that President Kaunda would not eat meat until the rest of Zambia's citizens could afford to do so.) On leaving Macha, an accident left the Commissioner of Police with a broken pelvis. He received such good care at Macha Hospital that he refused to be moved to a large hospital.

The second event was the grand opening of Muchila, one of some twenty-five clinics serviced by Macha Hospital. David would take his turn in caring for patients there.

The Nature of the Byers' Work

Early in his work at Macha, David commented: "Certainly there is enough to keep us busy here."[5] Letters to his parents (fortunately preserved by his mother) serve to substantiate his claim. They give us a glimpse into Zambian life and some of the health issues in the region (reference to malaria, however, is largely absent in the letters).

Leprosy was one of the issues he referred to several times in the letters. He treated lepers both at Macha and in the outlying clinics. In one letter he wrote that one day he saw 110 leprosy patients at Macha, and on another day about seventy-five.[6] At Namwala, one of the clinics, he saw approximately 120 patients, sixty of whom had leprosy. "I loaded as many [seriously ill] as I had room for [to take to Macha] and there should be more coming sometime."[7]

The disease obviously interested him, in part, because he resented the stigma attached to it. He addressed this issue in an article in the *Evangelical Visitor* entitled "Some Facts about Leprosy," written while he was at Macha. The article contains a detailed description of the disease. He pointed out that leprosy in most cases can be cured if patients take the right medicine. David believed that if people know the facts concerning leprosy, they would be less fearful of it and the disease would lose its stigma.[8]

Measles was another disease he encountered many times. In early 1968 he wrote that in the last two days the Macha Hospital had twenty cases of measles, and that more children in the area are killed by measles than by any other disease. But, as with leprosy, proper treatment (vaccination) can save many lives from the disease. At one clinic he visited, a near riot occurred because women were pushing to get the medicine before it was depleted.[9]

He delivered many babies, his work sometimes accompanied by cultural practices he did not know in the United States. In one of his first deliveries he did a C-section on a young girl, who, however, died from complications. David took the girl and her mother to their village twenty miles from Macha. "Her mother wailed all the way," the letter reads, "and when we got to the village, the women really cut loose, rolling...in the dust."[10]

On another trip, this time to a clinic, he picked up a woman who had been in labor for two days. "She delivered just as we got her into the car. The grandmother slapped my hands away when I unwound the umbilical cord from the neck so I let her take over.... In about 15 minutes I delivered it whereupon the old woman who was standing at the car began to dance with joy."[11]

He had a very serious problem with one delivery. During the procedure he prayed, "Lord, you got me into this—now get me out." The delivery was successful.[12] On another occasion, David delivered triplets. At that time Jeannie was pregnant with their first child. Commenting on the delivery of triplets, David joked, "We should have taken a picture [of the triplets] to send as *our* birth announcement."[13]

At one time, what David described as a "virulent flu bug" sickened many people. To treat the sickness, he provided a cough mix called linctus pholcodeine, "which has been going like hotcakes. I gave some to Velma Brillinger [a missionary from Canada] and she liked it so well. I'm sure it must be at least 90% proof alcohol."[14]

On another occasion, relying on the training his
mother-in-law had given him, he operated on what he
called "the worst case of eyelashes rubbing on the cornea
that I have ever seen. That guy is really happy today." After
David removed the patches on his eyes, "the man became
busy reading his Bible."[15]

As he had foreseen, his days were usually more than
full. "Yesterday we biopsied a mass from the head of a
young girl we suspect may have a Burkett's tumor which is
rather rare in Zambia. Also amputated the little finger of a
woman who was bitten by a [daughter with psychiatric
illness] about a month ago." On the same day he attempted
to come to the aid of an elderly woman "who has nothing
to do but lie on her back. I suggested we ought to find
something for her to do and one of the sisters said, 'Oh, Dr.
Byer. She can probably while away the time better than you
or me.' Well, she didn't sew or knit, or weave baskets, so we
had her make cotton balls and she was so tickled to have
something to do and now really pesters us to give her more
cotton when she runs out."[16]

On another day he delivered a baby, saw 110 leprosy
patients, operated on a boy who had a cyst on his spermatic
cord, and helped to launch the new pediatric ward. Typical
of his visits to clinics was the day he traveled 190 miles to
four clinics on extremely muddy roads.[17] In another letter
David writes: "With X-rays on Monday, surgery on
Wednesday and Friday plus clinics all day on Tuesday and
Thursday, you can understand that patients here in the
hospital complain that they don't see enough of me."[18]

Jeannie tells of other experiences involving her and
David. One patient saw some remaining mangoes high in a
tree. When he climbed the tree to get some mangoes, a
branch broke. He fell and ruptured his spleen. David and

other doctors removed the spleen and stopped the bleeding. Had he been in one of the outlying villages, he undoubtedly would have died.

Another patient with a fracture was told to stay in bed until his cast was hard and dry. But he could not resist the sunshine; he sat on the sidewalk and went to sleep. A trail of army ants invaded his cast and began biting him. But the cast had to remain on the leg; the hospital had used the last of its plaster. "We dusted a little insecticide into his cast, but the ants died with their jaws still clamped to his leg. Poor man!"

While David did his doctoring, Jeannie did her nursing until noon of the day she gave birth to a daughter whom they called Lois. Upon arriving at Macha, Winnie Worman had introduced her to her nursing responsibilities, including the "workings of the surgery department, and the scary, hissing, antique autoclave [instrument sterilizer]." Jeannie once tried to help a crazed patient whom she could not control even after giving him medication to calm him. Even with David's help the man went berserk, breaking furniture and windows, biting a man, and attempting to run away.

At the same time, Jeannie enjoyed her work and contacts with African people. But on occasion she became frustrated, as she related in an addition to one of David's letters: "I am really getting sick and tired of OBs [obstetrics]. We have been frantically busy at the hospital all day and evening, then get called out of bed all night for OBs. Don't care if I never see another one. Last night I was up all day for two nights and three days and then get called out of bed 7 times the next night. The nurses didn't find out any information about the patients they were calling about so I gave them what for in the morning. I don't think they will do it again."[19] That incident illustrates Jeannie's ability to take command of a difficult situation and turn it around.

For a period of four months during their time in Africa, David and Jeannie worked at the Mtshabezi Hospital in Zimbabwe. At first this was not exactly to their liking: home and friends were at Macha. But on arrival at Mtshabezi they were pleased by what they found there—a well-equipped hospital, a nice house in which to live, and a good garden begun by Dr. Roger Sider and his wife Joann who left as the Byers arrived to replace them. As a later chapter will show, they were pleased to return to Macha where they were met with celebration.

8

Personal and Relational Experiences at Macha

Mission Life

From their letters and personal accounts, it appears that the Byers lived an interesting and enjoyable life in Zambia. Surely this is evidence of the ease with which they could adapt to cultures other than their own.

They lived in what Jeannie has described as a nice four-bedroom house. Living with them in the house were Sharon Miller and two 1-W young men, Ted Mitten and Alan Stutzman. Jeannie admits that "it took some getting used to working at the hospital and taking care of meals and laundry for all five persons living in the house." Fortunately all were "easy going and didn't criticize my amateurish efforts at housekeeping and cooking."

She insists that the five people enjoyed life together, despite—or because of—Ted and Alan's proneness to pranks. "One day," she wrote, "the guys killed a green mamba, a highly poisonous snake. They thought it would be fun to tease me by coiling it through the shoes on the front porch. I got close before I saw it, and remembered I had just passed a large stick. I approached the snake again and flipped its head which just flopped onto the floor. They were disappointed that I didn't freak out. I was happy that they didn't know how fast my heart was beating."[1]

Although life was relatively comfortable for them, they missed some items available in the United States. Several months after their arrival at Macha, David wrote to his parents asking them to send Koolaid, Good Seasons salad dressing mix, chives, chip dip mix, maple flavoring, food coloring, one bag of baggies, Doublemint and Dentyne chewing gum, cake and frosting mixes, pepperoni pizza mixes, and two window squirters. A tall order but it duly arrived, whereupon Jeannie made a cake which, typical of their generosity, they shared with friends. "We have been enjoying everything," she informed the Byers.

David and Jeannie turned their hands even to practical maintenance. David told his parents that in the last several evenings he and Alan Stutzman painted the hallway of the house in which they lived. The painting was necessary because one of the previous 1-W men had bounced a superball against the walls, which left very visible marks. "It was fun to paint and we are thinking of going over to the Manns [Roy and Esther] and painting their house." A few months later Jeannie installed twenty-two switches and plugs in the new pediatric building.[2] On a return trip to Africa in the mid-70s, David did electrical wiring for the nurses residence.

As David had fished in Ethiopia, so he also did in Zambia. He described one of his fishing experiences in a letter to his parents. "[At Namwala] I saw patients from 2-4 p.m. then [friends] Frank and Barbara [Dall] and I went fishing in the Kafue [River]. We caught 17 fish in about an hour. I wasn't especially eager to fish but suggested it as I knew Frank would like to go. He was quite impressed as I landed what he said was the biggest pike he had seen there.

I didn't even lose a lure in the branches along the river. We were out there until sundown which was very pretty."[3]

The next month he went fishing again in the river, and hunting with Graybill Brubaker. They shot a wildebeest which they unsuccessfully tracked for eight hours, then finally returned to the Mission.

Travel

The Byers enjoyed traveling in Africa, as all visitors to Africa do—to parks, other hospitals and missions, and elsewhere. A favorite trip was to the rural hospital at Namwala, stopping at clinics along the way. "We liked to take a wide-mouth thermos filled with homemade ice cream," Jeannie recalls, "which ensured an invitation to a meal at the home of British teachers.... Sometimes we stayed at the government guesthouse. There was a cook there who made delicious corned beef hash." The Byer household continues to eat "Namwala Guest House Hash."[4]

South Africa beckoned them, where, in the spring of 1969 they took a camping trip in a Volkswagen van, packed with a tent, cooking supplies, and four 1-W men (Ted Mitten, Ray Heisey, Dave Kipe and Ron Book). Their travel took them, among other places, to the famous Zimbabwe ruins, and to camping on a Boer farmer's grounds (the area's campground was occupied by South African troops on maneuvers). They spent several pleasant days in Kruger National Park, saw the huge planted evergreen trees of Swaziland, visited a Nazarene hospital, and saw the special wing of a hospital reserved for the many queens of the king of Swaziland.

Not least, Jeannie had the opportunity to pilot a plane again. However, the license that she obtained in Kansas was not valid in Zambia. So she obtained a Zambian license, after practice at Choma in a Cessna 150 plane, like the one she flew at Wichita. Now on the South Africa trip, at Durban she went for a one-hour flight. The plane, she wrote, "really took off in a zip.... There was a 10 mph wind right down on the strip and the plane really had a lot of go."[5]

Travel in Africa could have unexpected moments. While at Mtshabezi Hospital in Zimbabwe on their four-month assignment, the Byers made a shopping trip to Bulawayo. Heading home with a van full of goods and a barrel of gasoline, the vehicle ran out of fuel. They had a large amount of gasoline, but how could they get some of it into the van's tank? David took his stethoscope apart, used it to siphon some gasoline into a plastic shopping bag, then poured the contents into the fuel tank. Although they arrived home, the stethoscope was never the same again.

Other Relationships

Visits from both sets of parents added pleasure to David and Jeannie's African experience. Jeannie's parents arrived in October 1969. During their three-week visit, Jeannie's father did some odd jobs around the hospital; her mother did some of the cooking. "We enjoyed some delicacies," David reported, "which we usually don't have time to prepare."[6]

David's parents arrived in early 1970. They had planned to visit Israel on their way home, but Everett's mother died while they were in Nairobi, Kenya. Everett and Adela flew to California to be at the funeral.

Among friends that the Byers made beyond Brethren in Christ circles was Father Tuck, Chaplain of St. Marks boys school, whom David described as an Anglican high clergyman. While visiting in Mapanza, David and Jeannie attended a service at St. Anne's Anglican Church, officiated by Father Tuck. Ever curious to experience something new and to explore it, David talked with Father Tuck later. "We asked him afterwards what all the incense burning was for—the smoke got pretty thick—and he confessed he didn't know for sure—but he wants to do away with the practice as soon as possible as he always gets a headache [from it]."[7]

The two men became good friends. Father Tuck looked forward to fishing with David. The friendship continued long after David and Jeannie had returned to the United States. David reported also meeting the Anglican bishop in Lusaka on two occasions. To David he seemed "like a very nice person."[8]

Among the Byers' experiences in Zambia was the birth of Lois on August 8, 1970. Understandably, Zambians were excited about the birth. Shortly after Lois was born, David was talking with some Ila tribal people at the fires on the Mission grounds. They all wanted to come to see Jeannie and the baby. David selected an old matriarch to represent them all. The old woman pried open the baby's clenched hands, put a shilling in each hand, then kissed her on the forehead, leaving an ashy smudge.[9]

Another visitor to the new baby was Esther Mwaanga (Bina Ezra), the housemother at the student nurses dorm. She was very perturbed when she learned that neither David's mother nor Jeannie's mother was there to welcome their first grandchild. She appointed herself as grandma. She retained that title and a close relationship with the Byer family over the years until her death in 2014.

The actions of these two African women suggest the warm relationship that the Byers had with African people—a relationship that was reflected in other ways. John and Esther Spurrier relate that at times David would disappear; eventually he would be found sitting with people at the relatives' waiting shelter, practicing his Tonga and visiting with the people, much as he did with the Ilas from around the Namwala area, as noted earlier.[10]

One year he walked from family to family, distributing Christian calendars. This served a double purpose—to meet Zambian people and to promote good health. The calendars, he wrote, "have several pictures emphasizing eating a chicken a week, an egg a day and [drinking] a glass of milk a day. There is a picture of a child with marasmus surrounded by beer bottles and a slogan, 'The choice is yours—development or drink.'" By January 6, he had handed out about 150 calendars and planned to order 500 more. [11]

He recorded some special visits with Africans that show his attempts to understand African culture. On a trip to Namwala to treat patients, a polygamist invited him to sleep overnight in his home. "I thought it would be interesting," David reported, "to be able to say that I had stayed overnight with a polygamist…. He talked about many things in about four hours. He was wound up like a gramophone. I was a good listener."[12]

On another trip to treat patients, this time at the Muchila clinic, he planned to see Chief Muchila. "He is a nice old guy and is a sort of buddy of mine…. [One] time he was having malaria and when I told him I had the same thing the week before he said, 'Give me the same medicine that you took.'"[13]

On another occasion he had an extended conversation with a Zambian on witchcraft. A leprosy patient told him he could not sleep at night because of the actions of his ancestors. He had gone to a witch doctor who identified the person bewitching him—a hospital employee. The man came to David to discuss his problem; a long discussion followed. To the man's question of whether David believed in witch doctors, David diplomatically and with some understanding of the enormity of the issue for Zambians replied that he did not but he realized that it was a very real thing for the questioner. "I encouraged him to trust in God, as I believed that witchcraft was the work of the devil." Following the discussion, David had a long conversation with Sampson Mudenda, a Brethren in Christ Zambian minister, who told him that when someone dies "the African always thinks of *who* caused it rather than *what* caused it."[14]

A telling incident that illustrates the Byers' relationship to Zambians is the time that David insisted on taking an African boy to Lusaka to receive treatment that was not available at Macha. Around the same time, he did the same for the child of a missionary couple. But the Byers were criticized by some of the staff for doing the same for the black boy as for the white child. David's comment to his parents on the criticism was that he and Jeannie are considerably more pro-African than some white people.[15]

David preached several sermons while in Zambia. One was a funeral sermon for a little girl named Sophia, an epileptic who died from severe burns. To be asked to preach this sermon was surely a sign of the empathy that he had for his African friends.

Africans at Macha reciprocated the affection. In one letter to his parents, David wrote that "the Macha people are much more friendly and grateful than Americans, that is for sure."[16] When the Byers left Macha for four months of service at Mtshabezi in Zimbabwe, both Macha people and the Byers were sad. The Byers much preferred to remain at Macha because of the many friends they had there. Their return to Macha from Mtshabezi was different: David wrote that as they were unloading their car, "pandemonium broke loose in the trainees' living area. They had caught sight [of us] and were jumping up and down for joy! It really was something."[17]

The Byers' attachment to Zambia and to Macha in particular is caught in another of David's letters. "I dare say," he wrote, "if I were not returning to America for training I would prefer to remain here where I would feel I could have something to do with the shaping and training and molding of a nation."[18] The following month, after having read President Kaunda's *A Humanist in Africa*, he thought that if they returned to Africa, he may want to work for the government.[19]

As the following chapter will show, Africa remained a very significant element of David and Jeannie's lives even though living and following a career in the United States.

9

More of Africa

Return Trips to Macha

David and Jeannie's two terms of service—one in Ethiopia, the other at Macha—did not end their interest in Africa. The earlier service inspired a continuing interest in and support of Christian ministries on the continent, especially at Macha.

The Byers returned to Macha in January 1975 where David again worked in the hospital. By this time, with three children now in the family, Jeannie no longer did nursing. She was, however, much involved in the life of the community.

Esther Dourte Spurrier and her husband John arrived at Macha from the United States during this time, he to join the medical staff as a physician in the hospital. Esther recalls Jeannie's valuable help in introducing her to the people and culture of the community. After observing that the Byers "were a great resource to help us orient to life in a new cultural community," Esther relates that "Jeannie took me to my first Tonga funeral—the most important event in this society—and taught me what to do and say. I still remember who died (Bina Josephine) and what the village looked like."[1]

Esther was impressed with Jeannie's comfort in the Zambian culture. "She modeled ease and assurance in raising her children here.... Her stories of her childhood as a child of missionaries were always entertaining and sometimes instructive.... They developed deep friendships with Zambian families."

Unfortunately, in contrast to the Byers' first term at Macha, David's subsequent letters to his parents were not preserved, thus fewer details of his work during this second, shorter term are available. In addition to medical activities, David wired the new nurses residence for electricity.

A third, one-month trip to Macha for the Byers came in 1977. Accompanying them were Jeannie's Aunt Esther whom they left in Ethiopia to visit Jeannie's father, Chuck (her brother) and Mary Alice Jordan. At Macha David substituted for Doctors Phil Thuma and John Spurrier while they were on vacation. He also was one of the speakers at the tenth anniversary graduation of Zambia Enrolled Nurses Training School at Macha. On their return to the United States, the Byers stopped at Addis Ababa in Ethiopia where they visited with Jeannie's parents and Arlene Schuiteman, and picked up Aunt Esther.

After this trip, travel to Africa temporarily ended. The demands of David's work at Mayo Clinic and caring for a growing family (eventually six children) seemed to make another trip to Africa impossible.

But eventually the family did return to Macha. In large part, this was owing to the children's interest in the people and places their parents talked about. Their son Paul describes this interest: "I have many memories of the fascinating stories my mother would tell of her adventures growing up in Sudan and going to school in Egypt—lions, witch doctors, poisonous snakes, hardship.... In addition to this were their stories of great care for the people they were there to serve, and of the people who changed their lives."[2]

One of the stories Paul recalls was that of a little Zambian girl who was struck by a mission vehicle when she darted from the tall grass. Her head was badly injured; her brain was bleeding and causing severe pressure. David ran to a tool shed and obtained an ordinary carpenter's drill since the hospital had no surgical drills. After sterilizing it he drilled into the girl's head, which relieved the pressure. After a month in a coma, the girl recovered completely.

Another story Paul says the children liked to hear was the time their father was returning from visiting clinics. At a village someone had loaned him a bicycle and another person had given him some eggs. In going down a hill, he discovered that the bicycle had no brakes. He crashed into a ridge of gravel made by a road grader, and was knocked unconscious. Blood flowed and the eggs broke. The chief's daughter, in a passing bus, recognized him as a doctor at Macha Hospital. They stopped, picked him up, covered with blood and eggs, and took him to Macha. Later David realized that sometime between the crash and his return to consciousness, someone stole his watch.

What children would not be interested in such stories and wish to see the places where they occurred?

Given this interest, the parents took the children to Macha in 1995. Thereafter the Byers made at least one annual visit to Macha until in the most recent years health problems prevented them from doing so. When David could accompany the travelers, he helped to administer anesthesia in the hospital. Jeannie helped to organize donated medicine and supplies that the Byers always brought with them.

On one trip, the Byers arrived at Macha at 4 p.m., after two days and one night of travel, too tired to begin the inventory of the medicine they had brought. "We did not know that the hospital was completely out of spinal anesthetic. Next morning when we went to the pharmacy [to unpack the medicine], we were greeted by a person from the operating room, who knew that we had brought the needed medicine. A patient was already on the operating table waiting to be given the anesthetic."

The family's trips to Macha were always joyous occasions. The Byers thought of their trips as "going home." Among their activities were visits with Bina Ezra in her village of Bulebo, sometimes celebrating her birthday with her. At least two of the children spent a weekend in the village, an experience that one son claims was an important event in his life.

This suggests that trips to Macha never became routine. As late as 2011, Jeannie wrote of their time in Macha in February of the previous year. "We had a great time visiting friends who are like family to us. We celebrated the 80th birthday of Bina Ezra, who appointed herself grandmother to Lois when she was born in 1970. We had a nice party with her in her village. Dave was in a lot of pain with his back but still managed to get to the hospital to give some anesthetics and visit a nearby church started by our friends Abraham and Vera Mhango. We gave Bibles from the Salem Road Covenant Church kids to the Bible Quiz team at the Lupata Brethren in Christ Church."[3]

David's children were observant of their parents' relationship with the Zambian people. Paul notes that his father's favorite activity, after working in the hospital, was to go to visit at "the fires" (where relatives of patients camped and cooked meals). "He and I went down several times and just chatted with folks there because my father has always been intrigued by interesting characters and places."[4]

Paul's observation of his parents' relationship with Zambians is confirmed by Dr. Sam Brubaker who was visiting surgeon at Macha on one of the Byers' later visits. "David took time to help me experience various aspects of African life, and took me to visit several outpost rural clinics. I have vivid memory of a non-clinical visit to a village comprised of a headman and his several wives and their children. We had a lengthy visit, learning this man's approach to producing and storing a supply of food adequate for the needs of the village—he strove to have at least a year's supply in reserve, so as to be able to survive a year of complete crop failure.

"I was impressed by David's interactions with Zambian people, whether hospital staff workers or patients. I observed him to be friendly and respectful. Particularly notable was his demeanor—non-pretentious, informal, casual, and non-authoritarian. He expressed this demeanor by giving time to converse with Africans; by allowing them to inform him; even by wearing very casual clothing, which displayed none of the customary insignia of medical professionals nor indicators of western affluence."[5]

These later trips to Macha frequently included more than family members. Sometimes they took members of their congregation at Rochester and personally paid their expenses. This was a conscious effort by the Byers to introduce friends to a culture other than their own, thus to expand their horizons beyond their own country and local communities.

Medical Supplies

On all their trips to Macha they took medical supplies. They also took medical supplies to Ghana for Africa Partners-Medical. This organization was initiated by Lewis and Rosebud Roberts, a couple in the Byers' congregation, both medical doctors from Ghana. Jeannie packed the supplies and arranged for team members attending conferences in Ghana to carry them as their checked luggage. The suitcases contained equipment to be used in the conference seminars, the supplies to be distributed to various places in West Africa.

Transporting medicine to Ghana and Macha was no small accomplishment. The work of collecting, packing and shipping unused medicine and other medical supplies was largely Jeannie's responsibility, although in the process others assisted her.

Son Paul has described the procedure as it relates to Zambia. "Macha would send us a list of needs and my mother would go to a convent in Rochester that received the overstock items from Mayo Clinic. She would bring home what she could find and take it to the old playroom which became the sorting room, organize and pack it into suitcases. I would often help by rolling gauze bandages, packing items into zip locks and weighing suitcases. She was so strategic about how things would fit (where and how) in order to pack the suitcases right up to the weight limit for checked baggage. Each traveler would get to take two of these suitcases. We put our personal items into our carry-on luggage.

"We could then try to make it through customs without declaring anything, since they [customs officers] never could understand that the supplies were free to us and we were giving them away. My mother, in her typical organized and prepared fashion, would present letters from Mayo and letters from Macha stating our intentions when we were confronted. I do not remember any time not getting through customs—eventually."

Many suitcases would go on each trip, usually numbering in the twenties, forty-four on one occasion. They were typically old suitcases, costing little or nothing, and were of different colors. No two suitcases were identical. They were all numbered and described (such as by size, color, brand, weight), and their contents itemized, allowing for easy identification. Jeannie excelled at collecting old suitcases from members of her congregation.

Part of the process was prayer. In a presentation to a Sunday school class in her church, Jeannie told the members: "I pray for each suitcase, the team [going to Ghana], for people who will be using the supplies, for the patients who will benefit, for safe travel for the luggage. Nothing has been broken or lost on the way," although sometimes that was not the case for items, such as souvenirs, that they brought home with them.[6]

Three Friends from Africa

Another way in which the Byers maintained their contact with Africa was through individuals, as illustrated in the stories of three of their friends.

One was Arlene Schuiteman. A nurse, she had worked near Jeannie's parents in Southern Sudan. As noted earlier, the Byers had visited her when they were in Ethiopia where she served as an instructor at a dresser training school. She recalls on that visit that one morning David and Jeannie slipped into the classroom and sat in the back row where they could observe what was taking place while she was teaching the class. It was, she adds, part of the keen way in which they observed life.

Because of political conditions in Ethiopia, Arlene returned to the United States in 1977. Later she and the Byers met in Sioux Center, Iowa. She has related how that meeting led her to go to Macha. "One day I received a phone call from Janet Groff, David's sister. The Byers were coming to visit Janet. Jean remembered that this was my home town and she wanted to get in touch with me. So Janet invited me to have lunch with them.... That afternoon David set up his projector and began showing slides. The slides were of Macha Hospital in Zambia. They showed the student nurses in their uniforms and patients in their hospital beds. This reminded me afresh of the work and the people I had left, and I was still longing to return to Africa.

"That day a seed was planted in my heart. I did not know it at the time, but there was an urgent need for a tutor at the Nurses Training School in Macha. Dr. Byer, who was aware of the need, was led to Rev. Glenn Bruggers, the Reformed Church in America representative of our mission work in Africa. The situation in Ethiopia did not improve, so I was encouraged to apply for the need in Macha. I was accepted to be the Director of Macha Nurses Training School."[7]

It should come as no surprise that the Byers took Arlene to Macha at their own expense. Thus again David and Jeannie served Macha well.

A kind of postscript to Arlene's years in Africa and her relationship to the Byers came some time following her retirement from Macha and return to Sioux Center. Beginning in 2006, Jeff Barker, a theater professor at Northwestern College in Orange City, Iowa, produced two plays centering on Arlene's life in Africa—"Sioux Center Sudan," and "Iowa Ethiopia."

David and Jeannie were impressed by these plays. They recommended to Barker a third play based on Arlene's life at Macha. The Byers financed an exploratory trip to Zambia for both Arlene and Jeff. This resulted in the production of a play entitled "Zambia Home," which featured two major problems—AIDS and malaria. A fourth play, entitled, "Arlene: An African Trilogy," combined elements of the former three plays. In the script of the last two plays, David had what he called a "cameo appearance."[8]

Another person who provided a continuing relationship with Africa was Bina Ezra, the self-appointed grandmother to the Byer children. The Byers' visits with her in Zambia were reversed when on two occasions, both for health reasons, Bina Ezra lived with the Byers in their home in Rochester.

She came to Rochester in 1999 for knee replacement surgery, accompanied by her African nurse, Julian Sikalima. Before surgery she was able to attend the wedding of "granddaughter" Lois to Joe Caffrey. After Bina Ezra's recovery, Jeannie took her back to Zambia, accompanied by two friends, Arlene Schuiteman and Doris Bjaastad.

Two years later the Byers received an email from their son Brian, doing malaria research at Macha, saying that Bina Ezra was seriously ill from an injury that caused infection in one of the replaced knees. Jeannie flew to Lusaka to bring her friend back to Rochester, taking with her two suitcases of medical supplies for Macha. This time Bina Ezra attended the wedding of a second grandchild, Elaine, to Joel Heuton. Needless to say, the Byers personally financed these trips.

Following each hospitalization, Bina Ezra recuperated in the Byer home. She was a delightful guest, creating much happiness by her presence. The Byers and the two Zambians—Julian and Bina Ezra—joked about white people eating brown bread and brown people eating white bread. Bina Ezra and Julian liked to sit in the sunshine

(Rochester climate is colder than the Macha climate); the Byers would say to the two African women that they were trying to get a deeper tan. One day Bina Ezra asked Jeannie to make Zambian food for dinner. She said she was tired of eating with a fork; she wanted to eat with her fingers. At Elaine's wedding she and Julian joined in a duet to sing "Choolwe Cipati" ("Showers of Blessings"). The Byers' contact with Bina Ezra continued until her death in 2014 at the age of eighty-four.

Julian Sikalima is a third continuing contact with Africa. She is the daughter of Rev. Joseph and Jane Sikalima of Macha. He was in charge of hospital maintenance and she was the busy mother of seven children. She also made fritters that the children sold to hospital visitors and staff. Jeannie describes the family as "the most hospitable people we know, sharing even their last food with needy visitors. They are very humble and demonstrate God's love with all their actions." Their first children—Julian and Jaryn—are identical twins. They both graduated from Macha Nurses Training School of Zambia (similar to practical nursing). After graduation they worked on the staff of the hospital.

As noted, Julian accompanied Bina Ezra when the latter came to Rochester in 1999 for knee replacement surgery. Her role was to interpret, explain, and, in general, support Bina Ezra. While Julian was living with the Byers, daughter Elaine, a recent graduate of the Bethel College nursing program, suggested that it would be nice if Julian could study there too. The Byers took her to the Sylvan Learning Center for a test in English proficiency, which she passed, and which allowed her to enter Bethel College to study nursing. The Byers paid for her travel, tuition, books, and other expenses for the five years she attended the college. On vacations and holidays, Julian lived with the Byers.

On one of their trips to Macha, the Byers met a young doctor, Lottie Hachaambwa, who they thought would be a good match for Julian. The next time they went to Macha they took Julian with them to meet Lottie. The two young people married in 2006. Seven of the Byer family attended the wedding in Lusaka, Zambia; Elaine was a bridesmaid and Joel played his violin.

The newly married couple returned to the United States, Lottie to finish his internal medicine residency in Miamisburg near Dayton, Ohio, Julian to continue her nursing career. Later the couple moved to Rochester, New York, for Lottie's infectious disease fellowship. The couple, now with daughter Tite, then returned to Zambia. Lottie works for the University of Maryland and teaches at the University of Zambia Medical School. The Byers have visited them when in Zambia. Lottie attended the memorial service for David in November 2014.

Julian, Lottie, and their family are among the fruits of David and Jeannie's generosity to and interest in people of another continent.

Other Support Activities

In various other ways the Byers have retained their interest in Africa, especially in Macha, and have been generous in their support of its programs. They have provided funds to support a Zambian to work in the Macha pharmacy to clean and maintain some order in the medications on the pharmacy shelves. For about twelve years they partnered with the building committee of the Zambian Brethren in Christ, chaired by Joseph Sikalima, to help finance the purchase of such items as door and window frames, and roofing material for church building projects. They also provided the capital outlay for the hammer mill at Sikalongo Bible Institute, and made financial contributions to the malaria institute at Macha. Also in recent years they contributed children's books to a community center near the Macha compound. They had become interested in the special collection at Messiah College of original illustrations created for children's books. Their interest led them to a children's book entitled *Sense Pass King: A Story from Cameroon.*

David wondered how children in Zambia would react to the story and the illustrations. He took the book with him on one of their trips to Macha. The Zambian children were fascinated by the book (see the photograph of David reading it to the children in Bina Ezra's village).

Following that reading the Byers bought and sent books to the community center, mostly for children but some for adults. A major motive in doing so was to encourage good reading habits by Zambian children.[9]

Receiving from Africans

Finally, as may be gathered from the above account, the giving by the Byers was not one way. Their work and contacts in Africa provided a likely avenue by which they could work out their desire to help people. Their interest in cultures other than their own could be stimulated. And they could learn from African culture, as David was obviously doing by talking with Zambians at the fires near the hospital.

This learning from Africans may be specifically illustrated by David's regard for Elijah Mudenda. Mudenda received his primary education at Macha. He pursued higher education, eventually receiving two university degrees, one from Cambridge University in England. He entered politics in 1962, and when Zambia gained its independence in 1964, he was appointed Minister of Finance, later Foreign Minister, eventually Prime Minister in President Kenneth Kaunda's government.

David saw him twice—at Chief Macha's funeral and at Chilonga church where he briefly chatted with him after the service. David was impressed by the humility, sense of service, and loyalty to the Brethren in Christ Church that he observed in Mudenda. While visiting Moscow as Foreign Minister, Mudenda refused to drink vodka. He did not hesitate to proclaim himself Brethren in Christ. A highly placed man following such principles, David once said, was an inspiration and encouragement to hold to the Christian virtues that he espoused in his own life.[10]

10

Civic Interests

Contributions to City and State Life

Those characteristics that are apparent in people with strong political instincts have been largely absent in the Byers. Neither one of their backgrounds would have led them into significant political activity. Jeannie's parents, as missionaries and as foreigners in Africa for much of their lives, would have been forbidden to act out what political views they may have had. David's Brethren in Christ background until the mid-1950s would have discouraged holding public office much beyond school trusteeship.

David and Jeannie moved beyond that largely non-involvement to some interest and activity in more local civic life. The most aggressive political action that David took was to serve as treasurer in the electoral campaigns of Gil Gutknecht, first for the Minnesota House of Representatives, later for the United States Congress.

David volunteered to serve in this office following the then treasurer's move to a southern state. Gutknecht had earned David's respect when he was the only candidate to appear at a meeting held in St. Paul to discuss medical issues. David was attracted to that kind of attention to serious social issues.

He became treasurer of Gutknecht's campaign committee around 1988. As treasurer he tracked income and expenses and prepared, signed, and submitted the financial reports required by what is now called the Minnesota Campaign and Finance Public Disclosure Board. However, beyond these functions, David was not otherwise an active member of Gutknecht's committee, which usually met at a time when he was not able to attend because of his duties at Mayo Clinic. Thus he was not involved in the planning work of the committee.

David also supported Rochester City Councilman Robert Nowicki. In an election campaign, Nowicki's opponent accused Nowicki of being soft on crime, and cited crime rates in the city to prove his point. In a letter to the editor of the city paper, David wrote that he had known Nowicki for ten years and had served with him on the Mayor's Advisory Council of Neighborhoods. He was proud to continue to support his candidate.

A paragraph in this letter illustrates David's penchant for research. "He [Nowicki's opponent] tried to tell me my city taxes were up by 58% over five years. When I checked I learned ours were not anywhere near that amount. He tried to tell me that crime was up too. I haven't had a chance to check on that. Now he wants to raise the city's hotel-motel tax by another 4%. I expect that will be pretty hard on a lot of sick people visiting our city [for treatment at Mayo Clinic and other health facilities].... I don't think we should soak poor people with more taxes."[1]

Although David disagreed with Nowicki's opponent about tax rates and the severity of crime in the city, he recognized that certain improvements should be made, as in public safety. He became convinced that one way of reducing vandalism was to replace burned-out street lights. Over the years he reported hundreds of dead lights. "I'm not certain that my action prevented crime," he admitted, "but I had some satisfaction in being able to drive down Broadway with all the lights aglow."

David's pastor, Mark Evinger, gives an interesting description of David's effort to replace dead street lights. The pastor introduces the story by saying that David is one of those individuals whose mind is constantly going and has the energy to keep up with his thoughts. "One night one of our parishioners saw David's car parked at the side of the road and David standing beside it. The parishioner found a place to turn around to go back to see if Dave needed help. By the time he got there, Dave had moved on. However, he saw him stopped again a little further down the road. This time he caught up with him and asked if he needed help. Dave didn't need any help, he was just driving around town noting the street lights that were out and was writing down the lights' identification numbers in order to report them to the city. Who bothers about such things?"[2]

On another occasion David noticed suspicious behavior in the neighborhood. He recorded the license plate information on the car of the person he thought might be causing the trouble. A few days later, David was accompanying a police officer on his patrol when the officer's radio reported the arrest of the person owning the car whose license plate number David had reported.

Out of his concern for safety in his and other neighborhoods, in 1996 David helped to form an advisory committee to the mayor on how to strengthen neighborhood associations. A major accomplishment of the committee was the production of a handbook on city ordinances. "Two years ago," the city's newspaper reported David as saying, "I became upset with the violence in our community. The city needed to call attention to some ordinances, especially those relating to misuse of firearms and curfew times." Over four months and under David's leadership, the committee condensed 400 pages of city ordinances into twenty. The published booklet helped to clarify the guidelines for communities, answered frequently asked questions, listed resources to contact for information on housing, fire and crime prevention programs, and identified neighborhood watch groups and associations. The newspaper article noted that although the booklet is now published only in English, Byer says that he will work to have it translated into other languages as well.[3] A revised edition of the booklet is currently used by the city.

Peace Activities

Given David's concern about growing instances of crime in the city, a logical question to raise is how he would react if an act of violence were to be committed against him or his family. An answer, of sorts, is in the following account told by David, with an obvious note of humor. (He entitled the story, "Defenseless Follower of Jesus Deals with an Intruder.")

"It was a hot summer day," he told the author, "ideal for applying stain to cedar siding. In the evening I left the ladder leaning against the house, ready for the next day. The ladder was just before our open bedroom window. After falling asleep I was awakened by the sound of someone climbing the ladder. I crouched down and let out the most frightful roar I could muster. Jeannie awoke with her heart going pitter patter. We heard the sounds of a rapid descent down the ladder. When I explained to Jeannie what was going on, we were both convulsed with laughter."[4] Thus a potentially dangerous situation was avoided by peaceful, although loud, action.

David held strongly to his views on peace. The church into which he was born and reared, the Brethren in Christ, is one of the historic peace churches, along with Mennonites and other related groups. As noted, he served a few years in Africa as a conscientious objector. He would always remain a pacifist. His views on peace help to explain another of his and Jeannie's civic actions—support of the World Peace Tax Fund and of peace demonstrators.

The World Peace Tax Fund promoted congressional legislation that would allow the estimated share of one's taxes that were applied to military purposes to be used for peaceful ends. In 1984, David agreed to help coordinate promotion of the World Peace Tax Fund's work by being its coordinator in southeast Minnesota. He obtained the names of people in his district who were on the mailing list of the organization. He was surprised to find that his name was on the list but that it contained only sixteen other names. He prepared letters to send to these sixteen people, asking each to send him two other names as prospects for joining the organization. But he admitted they had a long way to go before they could persuade their Congressman that theirs was a cause worth supporting in the nation's Capitol.

Describing his work with the World Peace Tax Fund, David wrote about taking part in a Rochester peace walk (he refuses to call it a march, because that sounds too militaristic). The entire Byer family—parents and children—joined the walkers. "It was the first demonstration for all of us," he reported with a sense of satisfaction for something well done. After the event David and Jeannie made a monetary contribution toward the expenses of the walk.[5]

11

Church Life

Becoming Members of the Rochester Covenant Church

Before moving to Rochester, David and Jeannie attended services in a variety of churches. For David this began while a student at the University of Kansas, his first significant location beyond Brethren in Christ circles. While working as a student in a university science lab, a woman in the lab invited him to her Episcopalian church. He attended one service but was not impressed. Although he gave no reason for his negative impression, it may be conjectured that the difference in the style of Episcopalian worship from Brethren in Christ worship was a gulf too wide to leap at this time. Later, with a wider world view, that gulf would significantly narrow.

While still a student at the university, David attended other church services. These occasions included one or more times with Friends, Old German Baptist Brethren some twenty miles south of Kansas City, the Rainbow Mennonite Church, and the Roanoke Presbyterian Church. As noted, following their marriage, the Byers attended Covenant services at Hillcrest and later in Wichita.

On moving to Rochester, the Byers, now with Lois, began worshipping at the Rochester Covenant Church. Undoubtedly their earlier contacts with the Covenant Church inclined them in this direction. The more immediate influence came from Dr. Leroy and Eunice Steinbrecher whom the Byers had met in Zimbabwe when both David and Leroy were on the medical staff at Mtshabezi. The Steinbrechers had worshipped at the Rochester Covenant Church when Leroy was a surgical resident at Mayo Clinic. They recommended this church to the Byers, who acted on the recommendation.

There the Byers worshipped and there their first three children were dedicated in October 1974. However, they did not join as members. On their return from Zambia in 1976, they learned that the congregation would plant a church in the southwest part of the city, its place of meeting a school in the Country Club Manor. Given their sense of mission, the Byers considered this new church plant desirable and attended its services. After one year at Country Club Manor, the congregation bought property along Salem Road. To commit themselves to this new work the Byers joined the new Salem Road Covenant Church as members. Jeannie was the first member to sign the charter.

The Evangelical Covenant Church that David and Jeannie joined was in significant ways compatible with David's Brethren in Christ background. A brief description of the denomination's history as given by fellow church member Eugene Hokanson shows this compatibility. The denomination is an offshoot of the Swedish Lutheran Church, the division occurring as a result of revivals in the mid-nineteenth century. Most Covenant congregations are found in areas originally settled by Swedish immigrants. "The Church is pietistic and emphasizes a living personal life with Christ. The denomination is a 'free church' which holds fast to the core beliefs of Scripture but also allows freedom in those doctrines not essential to salvation. When presented with differing interpretations, Covenanters have always asked 'Where is it written?' Variation could be allowed if solidly backed by Scriptures." Hokanson illustrates this last element by showing that the congregation accepts conscientious objectors as full members in good standing, yet the current youth pastor of Salem Road serves in the Armed Forces.[1]

Contributions to the Church

A list of some of their responsibilities shows that the Byers have been very active in the life of the Salem Road Church. At various periods of time, Jeannie has served on both the hospitality committee and as a Sunday school teacher. David also taught in the Sunday school. He was a member of the first council of the Salem Road congregation, and frequently served terms as chairman of the council. He led at least two pastoral search committees (one for the senior pastor, another for a youth pastor). As Mark Evinger, the long-time current pastor, points out, David served in nearly every leadership position in the congregation.[2]

The Byers were active participants in the congregation in many other ways. They contributed generously to its operational expenses. David has said that the congregation never ended the year with a budget deficit; it may be assumed that the Byers had considerable to do with this positive outcome.

More tangible contributions were numerous. One was the paving of the parking lot. Eugene Hokanson describes the original parking lot as a grass field, which, after rain and the impact of the tires of many cars, became a muddy field. Research-minded David, "keeping his eyes open for things that would benefit the church," discovered the Oldham Little Church Foundation. Founded by Morris Oldham, a Christian businessman in Texas, the Foundation gives grants to small evangelical churches to help complete their facilities. Acting for the congregation, David obtained a grant sufficient to pave the parking lot.

Sometimes manual labor was part of the Byers' contributions to the congregation. In their Christmas letter of 2001, they reported that they had spent some time "mudding" sheetrock at the church's new Youth and Family Ministry Center.

Buying stained glass windows for the congregation's multi-purpose room was a project of which the Byers were justifiably proud. In 1984 David learned that two nearby Moravian congregations had merged; much of the furniture of one of the buildings would be sold at auction. He invited his friend, Eugene Hokanson, to accompany him, which the latter did because he "always enjoyed a good time with Dave."

Hokanson tells the story well, and in doing so gives further insight into David's character. "When we got to the auction it became apparent that Dave was interested in the stained glass windows [for the Salem Road church]. At the time there was no place to install the windows, but the congregation was growing and we had plans to expand. David visualized buying several of the stained glass windows ultimately to be incorporated into the new building."

The auction began, and bidding on the windows was vigorous. "Dave had won a couple of rounds and lost a couple, when a window featuring a bunch of grapes and commemorating the Lord's Supper came up. As Dave began to bid against a determined opponent, I offhandedly mentioned that the other guy was probably looking to hang it above a bar in his home. At that point Dave's demeanor changed. It was no longer, 'Well, I'll get some and lose others.' Instead it became 'I *shall* get this one.' Although the winning bid was something like double the price of the other windows, Dave got it. All told, he ended with four windows.

"For several years the windows languished in a church storage closet, but when the new building was designed, the windows were incorporated into the design, and they now beautify the east wall of the sanctuary. They are a testimony to Dave's love of the Lord."

And they were also an inspiration to David. In one of four devotional articles that he wrote for the congregation in 1985, he reflected on one of the windows and its meaning to him. "The largest window contains an illustration of the Paschal Lamb. The window catches the rays of the morning sunlight and transforms them into beams of white, purple, and brown. As I study the window I am reminded of sin and its cure.... Sin has a very specific cure. God's grace has been revealed to us through the presence and death of Christ, our Paschal Lamb. There is no other cure for sin."[3]

Providing transportation for church members and other people was a marked feature of the Byers' church life. Taking youth to camp and Bible quizzing, and encouraging members and staff to accompany them on trips for which the Byers drove their car are also illustrations of their generosity and help on a practical level. In fact, they always held a car in reserve for use in church-related activities, which was appropriately referred to as the "missionary car."

This generous loan of a vehicle may be illustrated in the following account related by Steve and Arlene Burgert. "In 2011, we sent out a letter to our supporters and prayer partners announcing an upcoming Home Ministry assignment in the United States for eight months in 2012. The Byers promptly replied that, of course, we would be free to use their car for all 8 months. They were not at all reluctant when we advised them we anticipated our travels would be for more than 10,000 miles. They said, 'We expect that.'"[4]

They went far beyond lending a car for such purposes; on two occasions they purchased cars for the ministerial staff. In 1980 the congregation obtained a new youth pastor who, as David put it, "needed wheels." On a trip to Minneapolis they noticed a Suburban for sale. "It seemed as if it had our youth pastor's name written on it." So the youth pastor obtained his "wheels" through the Byers' generosity.

Later, in 1996, a new pastor, Mark Evinger, arrived. His family was in need of a larger car. He has described how, unknown to him at the time, the Byers came to his rescue and provided a vehicle. In a letter to the Byers years later, he recalled how they had helped his family with a free vehicle: "It was a real blessing to my family. It relieved the stress of being a single-vehicle family consisting of three adults and two teenagers crowded into a small SUV.

"Did you know the night before [the Salem Road congregation] contacted me to candidate that we had a minivan that I took to a car dealer in Canada to sell on consignment, that the dealer sold the van, then promptly went bankrupt without paying me for it? We still owed a lot of money on the van but now it was gone, so we had a payment but no vehicle.... I decided to leave it in the Lord's hands and not pursue it, hoping that something good would come from it even though it was a financial burden I didn't want. Little did I know that a year later someone [the Byers] would be giving us a van."[5]

To the Byers' purchase of cars for church staff was added financial assistance to a youth pastor in buying a house. On being called by the congregation, the pastoral couple, Jeremy and Kari Bowers, began searching for a house. "We thought we might be able to help them," David later modestly related. "I suggested giving them $10,000. Jeannie wanted to know how much we paid for Pastor Mark Evinger's vehicle. That was $22,000. 'And what about the Suburban?' she asked. That was $18,500. After further discussion we settled on $20,000 to give toward the purchase of the house." Other church members also contributed money to the Bowers, thus lowering mortgage payments. Such generous giving by the Byers was made possible by simple living.

Discussing sermons with the pastor was still another way David engaged in the life of the congregation. Pastor Evinger relates that "occasionally David would say 'Your sermon reminded me of a sermon I heard'...and then he'd list the date, name the preacher, town and church, etc., ... and asked if I'd like to see his notes. A few times I said, 'Yes,' and was astounded at the level of detail he had written. Pages of information about the trip, the flight into the city, where he had dinner, details of the streets he had walked, information about the church, the pastor or priest. It was overwhelming. That's when I began to realize that this man had an incredible mind."

Various people have commented on the nature of the Byers' service to the congregation. Pastor Evinger claims that he could go to them with any request and he could count on them for help. Whatever they did, according to Ron and Sheryl Peterson, was without show or desire for recognition. "The Byers," they write, "have modeled community and ownership through participation in the life of the church.... [As church chairman] David was always very thorough in dealing with any issue and would think of all the questions that needed to be asked in order to arrive at a decision or conclusion to an issue. Jeannie modeled ownership through her ongoing participation on the Mission Committee for many years. Most of all they operate without fanfare or publicity of any kind.... David was an encourager and supporter of the decisions of the church. He commented that it was the Spirit of love and unity that was more important than a program or building project."[6]

Continued Mission Work

From their congregational base, the Byers continued their support of missions. Their son Paul remembers the time a missionary visited Salem Road Church and an offering was taken for his work. By accident his father added to the check an extra zero. David noticed the mistake before releasing the check but thought, "Oh well, I guess God is telling me they need more."[7]

The Byers also continued mission work in their community. Jeannie tells of two encounters in which she reached out to foreign women, one a Muslim, the other a young Chinese student. Of the first encounter, Jeannie writes: "When our daughter Lois was manager at Jo Ann Fabrics, I heard one Muslim woman say to another Muslim woman in Arabic, 'Hurry up. We are going to miss the bus.' I told them if they wanted to shop longer I would be glad to give them a ride. They asked, 'How much?' I said that I had a big car and I was going anyway and they were welcome to join us, no charge. They did. I let them off at their hotels. I gave the English-speaking woman my phone number and told her I could help her another time.

"A day or two later she asked for another ride and I took her. She asked, 'Are you a Christian? They do this kind of thing.' I said I was, and Jesus had filled my heart with love and I wanted to share it."[8]

A second similar witness occurred with Wang Lu. "I had taken Julian, our Zambian 'daughter,' to take a test. An Asian girl was in a corner crying. I put my hand on her shoulder and asked if I could help her. She said she had left part of her ID at her dorm and couldn't take the test. I told her I would take her to her dorm. But, the girl said, her dorm was in Winona [forty-five miles away]. I told her that, no matter, I would take her there.

"We went home and got Bina Ezra, our African 'grandma,' went to Winona, and brought the girl back for her test. I invited her to our home after the test for some Zambian food. When I got home I asked Bina Ezra to pray for Wang Lu and Julian as they took their tests. All afternoon I heard Bina Ezra's voice raised in prayer (she doesn't know how to pray silently) and singing hymns. After dinner when I was taking Wang Lu to get her ride back to her dorm, she asked if I was a Christian. I said yes and asked if she would like to learn more."

Jeannie contacted Dave Dolan of the Covenant Chinese Ministries who sent Wang Lu a Chinese Bible, a study book, and a booklet of testimonies of mainland Chinese people. Jeannie adds, "She called me later and said she was now a Christian and in Bible study."[9]

Jeannie maintains that although not working in other lands, they can still do mission work in the context of the congregation, home, and community. "We are unable at this time to be at the ends of the earth. But we are able to financially support others, lend a car, pray for and encourage them.... There is still Rochester (Jerusalem), Minnesota (all of Judea), and USA (Samaria)."

An Ecumenical Spirit

While David and Jeannie were immersed in the life of the Salem Road Church, they were also interested in other religious expressions. David liked to read theology, which accounts for the many books in his library on this subject. In later years he began to study Hebrew.

His interest in various religions is illustrated by the three Buddhist alms bowls displayed in his home office. He found inspiration in the bowls: "It is said that Buddhist monks are entirely dependent on what comes to them via the bowls.... I have the alms bowls to remind me of dependence, in my case, upon God's grace."[10]

He was defensive of Muslims living in the Rochester area. He told a Sunday school class that to show his Christian attitude towards Muslims, he frequented the Somali coffee shop located near the mosque.[11]

Although he insisted on tolerance toward the Muslims, he once took exception to an article in the city paper written by a Muslim who maintained that Jesus was also a revered figure in his religion. In response, David wrote a letter to the editor saying that he was disappointed that the article failed to show the similarities between the Muslim faith and Christianity—to give him something to identify with Muslims. But, he added, to claim Jesus as only a good figure in history was to deny what Christians believed, namely, the divinity of Jesus and the truth surrounding the events in his life, including the resurrection.[12]

We have seen that while in Africa, the Byers had contact with Anglican clergymen, including Archbishop Oliver Green-Wilkison, and that in an Anglican service in Zambia David had difficulty understanding the use of incense. But beginning with those contacts in Zambia, David developed a growing appreciation for Anglican/Episcopalian services, which he sometimes attended when away from Rochester, such as All Souls Church in London, England, of which John Stott was pastor. In 1986, while attending a conference for anesthesiologists in New York City, he celebrated Pentecost Sunday with what he called "my charismatic Episcopalian friends."

His explorations of other modes of religious worship also took him to the Orthodox Church. In New York over one Easter, he went to an Orthodox Saturday service. Impressed, he wrote to his parents: "The Saturday morning liturgy lasted for three hours and included 15 lessons from the Old Testament recounting the mighty acts of God. For me the high point of the service was after about the 8th lesson when my friend Deacon Michael sang the song of Moses while the choir in the background sang 'Gloriously Has He Been Glorified.'"

"The Easter vigil," he continued, "began at 11:30 p.m. Saturday evening with the church in darkness. Everyone held a candle which was lit as fire was passed from person to person. That service lasted until about 2:30 a.m., and then everyone went to the refectory for the Easter feast."

Of these services David wrote, "I enjoyed my time with my Orthodox friends. I went so that I might experience the Orthodox celebration and think of my friend Father Nicolas."[13]

The unlikely friendship with a Russian priest is further proof of David's—and Jeannie's—interest in other faith traditions. On one occasion, Father Nicolas sent a cable to the Byers conveying Easter greetings from him and his family.

David expanded on this friendship with Father Nicolas in another devotional article he wrote for the congregation, entitled "Pray for Others." He informs his readers that for some time he has been praying for everyone on a personal basis, "including even a Christian in the Soviet Union. During the past year I have established contact with Father Nicolas, a Russian Orthodox priest. Our friendship has been a rewarding experience! We, as well as our teenage daughters, have exchanged prayers, gifts, and letters. Through our friendship I have learned to know two Russian Orthodox priests in the United States.

"On our fireplace mantel we have a picture of Father Nicolas, his wife, and their four children (Elena, Konstantin, Maria, and Anna). The influence of this picture on my thoughts about disarmament is best summarized in the words of Wendell Berry: 'Who has imagined your death negligible to me, now that I have seen those pictures of your face.'"[14]

When in New York, David liked to visit the Logos bookstore which claimed to have the largest selection of Judeo-Christian books and Bibles in the city. He visited the store on one occasion to view its collection of books on Eastern Orthodoxy.[15]

David also attended a few Roman Catholic services, including at St. Francis in Rochester. Undoubtedly he did not share in the Eucharist, but he was an interested observer. In describing to two Messiah College friends (Anita Voelker and Cherie Fieser) the Eucharist service he once attended, he used the word "wafer." "I received a good lecture from Anita [a Roman Catholic] who said, 'That is the *Host*, not a wafer.'"

In one of his devotional articles for the Salem Road Church, David commented on his ecumenical spirit. "Our family has had the privilege of worshipping God in a variety of settings. We have attended evensong in York Cathedral [England], worshipped with a Nuer congregation [Africa] in a mud and stick chapel, praised the Lord in a shrine inside a baobab tree, recounted the mighty acts of God in a Passover Seder, and participated in a service containing the world's fifth largest pipe organ. We have experienced the enthusiasm of black worship services and the quiet of a Quaker meeting. At Jasna Góra in Poland I have sensed the devotion of Polish people [the monastery is famous for its shrine to Virgin Mary and as a destination for pilgrims]. Jeannie's American accent has surprised Anglican worshippers in Norwich, England, as she read the lesson."[16]

In another place David claimed that he is as "perfectly happy worshipping with the Iowa Old Order River Brethren [a small conservative 'plain group'] as with St. Francis in Rochester [Roman Catholic]."

David recently explained to the author his interest in these faith groups. "I would have to say I am attracted to these varieties of worship styles because I like to worship the Lord. Secondly, I do like the people. Certain parts of the worship order thrill me. I like the phrase in the Nicene Creed that describes our Lord 'begotten not made.' Similarly I like the phrase from the *Book of Common Prayer*, 'He stretched out his arms on the cross, a perfect and obedient sacrifice for the sins of the whole world.' I think of the numerous accounts in Scripture of our Lord stretching out his arm(s) (hand) to minister to the people."

Brethren in Christ Connections

David's delight in meeting people of other faith traditions did not mean that he lost interest in the church of his childhood and youth. Becoming a member of the Covenant Church did mean that David severed formal ties with the Brethren in Christ, however reluctant he was to do so. But in requesting a transfer of membership in 1976 from the Pleasant Hill congregation, he explained that the closest Brethren in Christ congregation to Rochester was too distant for their active participation; this they could have in the Salem Road Church. Whatever discomfort he felt following this closure on his life with the denomination and particularly with the Pleasant Hill congregation may have been alleviated to a degree by the official closing of his early church home in the year following his transfer of membership.

In various ways David retained an attachment to the Brethren in Christ. Such historical beliefs of that denomination as peace, missions, simple lifestyle, and generously helping people were deeply engrained in both David and Jeannie. In later years they became strong financial supporters of Brethren in Christ-related Messiah College. David read Brethren in Christ literature. He became a life-time member of the Brethren in Christ Historical Society and, with the exception of a couple of issues, collected a complete set of the Historical Society's journal. He also collected many of the significant book publications of the denomination, including Carlton Wittlinger's *Quest for Piety and Obedience: The Story of the Brethren in Christ.* (When the author visited the Byer home in the spring of 2014, David proudly showed him his collection of journal issues and books on the Brethren in Christ.)

In David's travels, particularly in the eastern United States, he visited Brethren in Christ congregations. On a trip to Pennsylvania in 1977, he attended the denomination's Roxbury Holiness Camp meeting and worshipped on a Sunday morning with the Carlisle congregation (its pastor, Roy Wenger, invited him to his home for dinner). In another year David spent several days at the Memorial Holiness Camp meeting in Ohio, and at the same time joined Brethren in Christ ministers in a study course held on the campgrounds. And, as has been related, David and Jeannie participated in the denomination's missions program, both in medical service and ongoing financial support.

As late as 2014, the year of his death, David was still relating to the Brethren in Christ. In this year he wrote a letter to a professor at the Mennonite-related Fresno Pacfic University in which he referred to his and Jeannie's work at Salem Road and elsewhere. "But," he added, "at the same time we have maintained our interest in the Brethren in Christ Church. We remain loyal even though we are no longer members."[17]

12

Home Life

A Different Lifestyle

Throughout the years, David and Jeannie found pleasure and fulfillment in serving people. Driving expensive cars, living in a mansion, "keeping up with the Joneses," were concepts alien to their thinking. This disinterest in material things, beyond obvious necessities, freed them to serve people. As their daughter Lois states, "They both would prefer to help others than to spend money on themselves."[1] Friend Eugene Hokanson similarly comments, "They were always more concerned about helping others than looking for some kind of showcase."[2] They lived simply and gave generously.

Houses and Cars

Modesty describes the house into which they moved in 1976 following their time at Macha, and in which Jeannie continues to live with family members. The house became larger as the Byers added more rooms to accommodate a growing family and frequent guests (for whom they reserved a room). But even with additions, the house remained modest—in both its interior and external appearance.

Similarly with cars. They always owned more than one car—for their own family use and for the use of students, guests, and missionaries. But their cars and SUVs were not new when purchased, and they were driven well past the time that most owners would have discarded them. The Byers' cars are subjects of common comment by those who know them. David's brother Les claims that David enjoyed making good deals on used cars, and when the metal began to rust from the harsh condition of Minnesota winter roads, he took great pride in the use of duct tape on the rusting parts.[3] Eugene Hokanson tells of the Volkswagen Beetle that Jeannie bought shortly before her graduation. David bragged that the car had a "sun floor": the persons sitting in the driver's and passenger's seats could see the road under their feet. Lois recalls the time when she went with her father to Mayo Clinic to pack office items on his retirement. "We parked in the ramp reserved for doctors. I was surprised to see all the fancy cars parked there. My dad could have had cars like that but he preferred to use his money helping others and educating his children."

Hospitality

A steady stream of guests helped to characterize family life. They included Mayo Clinic patients (the Byer home served as a kind of Ronald McDonald house), families, students, missionaries, unwed mothers, friends, and family. Some guests remained for only a day or a night; other guests, such as students from other countries, stayed for longer periods. Some of their short-term guests discovered the Byer residence in *Mennonite Your Way* and in *Covenant Hospitality*. While these travel guides suggested that a small monetary fee be paid to the hosts, the Byers told their guests that any money they received would go to missions. In the Christmas letter of 1985, Jeannie wrote of guests who came to them from the guidebooks: "It is fun to meet these new people." According to Jeannie, all but four of them would be welcomed to return.

The Byers gave hospitality and parenting to many young people, many of them international, who came to the city for a variety of reasons.[4] Amir at thirteen years of age and Hamid at ten, both from Iran, were with the Byers for several months while they studied English. George from Poland and Boun Xou from Laos came to escape difficult political situations in their home countries. They knew no English. Both were with the Byers for four years. Nobu was an exchange student from Japan; he was in Rochester for a year to play football at the community college.

Other guests were Julian from Zambia, the Byers' "adopted" daughter, who when not in the nursing program at Bethel College, stayed with the Byers. Jessica from Canada had met David and Jeannie's son Paul when they were students at Covenant Bible College near Calgary, Alberta, Canada. A nursing student, she made her home with the Byers for two years. Clay Wagner from northwestern Pennsylvania came several times with his mother when he had heart surgery at Mayo Clinic. He lived with the Byers for two years because he found a job in Rochester that was not too strenuous for his heart. Ruan Albuquerque from Brazil was with the Byers for a few months while he studied at the community college.

George Greer from Poland may serve as an example of an international guest in the Byer home and the considerate treatment the Byers gave to those who came to live with them. David described George as "such a nice fellow." One evening, on their way to church, Jeannie gave George driving instructions. George had a penchant for neatness. He organized everything in his room, and often in the evening picked up the debris the children had left when they went to bed. The Byers enrolled him in school to study English and to benefit from testing and counseling.[5]

The Byers claimed that over the years as many as eighty people a year were their guests. Usually they accompanied the Byer family to church. "We never knew from one week to another," a church member commented, "who would be sitting with them in the second row, right side of the church, along with their extended family."

All of this hospitality the Byers saw not only as interesting and rewarding, but also and primarily as "Christian action."[6]

Rearing Children

Life with six lively children was both a delight and challenge to the parents. In disciplining their children, David and Jeannie took cues from their parents. This meant, among other things, that children should obey their parents. "If they didn't," Jeannie says, "they usually got spanked, or a privilege withdrawn. We had a list of house rules I would pull out…. We didn't give our children a lot of leeway. When they were little we painted red lines they were not to cross—one on the driveway and one behind the house. It was a big no no if they went some place and didn't tell us." She adds, in the spirit of many other older parents, "If we had it to do over again we wouldn't spank so much."

Discipline may have been relatively strict by current practices, but it was conditioned by a marked spiritual atmosphere. Externally this was evidenced by faithful church attendance, internally in a variety of ways. Lois remembers her mother "reading Bible stories to us at night, all of us sitting on the bed or floor or dangling from the bunks in the bedroom…. Our family devotions at dinner included reading Scripture and praying for missionaries."

In a presentation to his Sunday school, David described what the family is currently using in their devotional period. One source is the 1727 edition of *Conversations on Saving Faith for the Young,* written by one of his ancestors. They are also regularly reading from *Daily Light on the Daily Path.* And for prayer suggestions they follow the *Brethren in Christ Prayer Challenge* (listing mission needs) and the *Covenant Missionary Prayer Calendar.*[7] Singing was also part of family worship. A short time before his death, David in a letter to the author commented: "This morning at worship we sang, 'I Have Decided to Follow Jesus.' I teared up on the fourth verse as we sang, 'Will you now decide to follow Jesus?'"

Years earlier David was clearly pleased when little son Paul began to have a "serious interest" in saying table grace. "I think this coming Sunday I should suggest he may sit with me in church for 'big people,' and if he gets tired of it he can always go back to the nursery."[8]

An example of the Byer parents teaching spiritual and moral values is David's response to a letter that Brian received when he was a child. "Brian got a chain letter from a friend of his in British Columbia promising him a large number of postcards from interesting places, if he doesn't break the chain, so I think he is going to participate. We warned him not to expect too much and this may be a good way for him to learn to have some skepticism about promises too good to be true."[9]

Of increasing significance for the family was the celebration of Thanksgiving Day. Children, their spouses and their children, and other relatives came together year after year—as many as fifty-five, so large that the gatherings are now held in the church. David and Jeannie's

Christmas letters always comment on these events. In one of the letters Jeannie wrote that "it was a lot of fun.... The little cousins have a good time with each other. So do the big people!" In another she reports that thirty-four attended and the dinner was excellent. "It was very fun to see everybody. We are blessed by a great family."

To rear a family is seldom without difficulty, even (perhaps especially) for Christian parents. David and Jeannie had to deal with drug problems, especially with one teenager (see David's account of his depression in Appendix II). But he and Jeannie rightly did not accept the view that this was the fault of their parenting. In a letter to the city's *Post Bulletin*, David responded to an article in that publication in which the writer claimed that a major contributor to the problem of the use of methamphetamine is the lack of personal and parental responsibility. David labeled this view as "simplistic stereotyping." He wrote: "I speak from experience. My wife and I reared our six children to the best of our capabilities. Our children were a high priority in our lives. In three instances we dealt with substance abuse. We devoted the major portion of five years to dealing with these situations. We did not [as the earlier writer claimed] abdicate the raising of our children to society in general and school specifically. During treatment we met numerous parents facing similar problems.... We never met a parent who might be characterized as lacking personal and parental responsibilities."[10]

Travels

The Byers have been inveterate travelers. The family seems almost always to have been on the road—traveling to family (including David's parents in Kansas and Jeannie's in retirement in northeastern Tennessee), to Alaska, and abroad (see Jeannie's account in Appendix I). They went to such overseas countries as England, Scotland, Ireland, Zambia, Zimbabwe, Thailand (to Jeannie's brother David), to some of these countries multiple times. Many of the trips were related to conferences that David attended. In later years something of a tradition developed of traveling to London in January where David went to a conference and Jeannie celebrated her birthday and went shopping.

Of course, shorter trips were taken in the Rochester, Minnesota, area. Lois remembers her father taking her to fish at a trout farm, visiting an Amish buggy shop, touring a funeral home, and attending a farm auction. On such trips David often stopped at an ice cream shop to buy ice cream for the children, with instructions that the treat be finished before arriving home.

Sometimes the "outings" were more cultural in nature. In 1977 the family drove to Minneapolis to see the Children's Theater production of "Aladdin and the Magic Lamp." Years later David took Lois and her family to see "Oliver," performed at the Rochester Repertory Theater. Culture, of sorts, was absorbed when David in 1984 took young Brian and George from Poland to a demolition derby at the county fair. David reported to his parents that "Brian was all excited because four cars caught fire."[11]

All of these trips earned the family many frequent flier miles, and considerable mileage on the odometers of their cars. In one family Christmas letter, Jeannie wrote about the many miles their cars had gone. One was at 200,000 miles. Another car had to go to the junkyard but managed to make it under its own power.

A note, familiar to perhaps all parents, sounded in longer trips. "I'm thirsty," the children would say. Lois says that her father's standard reply was, "Swallow your spit."

He knew that too many beverages would result in "I need to go to the bathroom."

Personal Interests

Both parents had interests and diversions in addition to occupation and family. David loved books. Shelves lined with books covered a spread of subjects. Paul notes that "the house was perpetually stuffed to the gills in every room with books, books, books.... I remember sneaking into my parents' room and soaking in some of my father's collection of various tomes, from books on Rembrandt or Albert Schweitzer, and massive illustrated anatomy books."

David also loved music. As noted, while in Africa he liked to listen to the Mormon Tabernacle Choir and the Royal Philharmonic Orchestra. His tastes tended toward classical music.

He had some appreciation of art (see the chapter on Messiah College). He discovered Erin Maurice, an artist who made icons in the Coptic style. He and Jeannie purchased a couple of icons for their home and occasionally presented one to various friends (including the author whose icon depicts Jesus washing his disciples' feet).

David was also interested in genealogy. His work in this field built on and extended his father's work on the Byers. His genealogical searches led him to various locations and archives, including Pennsylvania and Ontario, Canada.[12]

According to Paul, his father was interested in old things, "both quality old fashioned objects and the people and stories and way of life that go with them. We planted an elderberry bush in our back yard to carry on his mother's tradition of making elderberry jelly. I remember that he owned various old-timey hats and that he restored his great-uncle's Victrola."

For a time David collected happy faces. Paul says that he had "smiley face ties which he wore during frequent flights to conferences and other events. The airline attendants and gate agents began to recognize him and he often got better service for it. He also got a neon smiley face for the window of his office which came on at twilight, beaming all yellow and happy."

Jeannie's interests were her growing family, providing hospitality, sending medical supplies to Africa, and traveling. She was also a talented seamstress, learning the skill while still a child in Africa. Paul notes that over the years she made many of his toys, Halloween costumes, clothes, backpacking gear for long trips, book bags, and jackets, which corresponded to the color (yellow, blue, pink, red, green or orange) that she gave to each child.

The Children[13]

Into the Byer home came six children, all of them well-loved, reared in the Christian faith, and given good educations. The birth of each child was a welcomed addition to the family. When the third child was born, David was accosted by a colleague at Mayo Clinic who asked him, "Don't you have enough children already? What about the world's overpopulation?" David's humorous reply was, "I thought about that and what I think the world needs is more people like Dave Byer." The following pages contain a brief snapshot of each child, in order of birth.

Lois was born at Macha in 1970. Along with Zambian and other white children she attended kindergarten taught by her mother. In Rochester, she attended the Jefferson Elementary School, Rochester Central Lutheran School and Lourdes High School. For her fourth year of high school she studied at Bethel College (now University) in St. Paul under the Post Secondary Enrollment Option (PSEO). At Bethel she majored in psychology and worked on an M.A. degree at St. Mary's University.

Following graduation Lois had successive positions as manager of a fabric store, showroom person at a plumbing supply store, and sales clerk at a clothing store. In New Hampshire she met Joe Caffrey on a visit to her college roommate; they married in 1999. Their daughter, Vanessa, was born in 2004. Lois now home-schools Vanessa, and Joe works at Mayo Clinic.

Brian was born in 1973 in Rochester. Like Lois he attended the Jefferson Elementary School, Central Lutheran School and Lourdes, learned to play trumpet and was a member of the high school band. After graduating from Bethel College as a pre-med student, he worked for two and a half years in Washington, D.C., in the office of local Congressman Gil Gutknecht on whose election committee David served as treasurer. He attended the University of Des Moines as a medical student, and spent the last quarter semester at the malaria institute in Macha.

Brian did his anesthesia residency at Mercy Hospital in Pittsburgh, Pennsylvania, where he met Sharon Smith, a corporate executive, whom he married in 2005. At the end of Brian's residency the couple moved to Duluth, Minnesota, where he serves as an anesthesiologist at St. Mary's Hospital. He also works in that role in Superior, Wisconsin. Their three boys are named Grant, Joshua, and Nathan.

Elaine was born in 1974. She attended the Lutheran school and John Marshall High School, in both schools playing the flute in the band. She also attended Lourdes where she became interested in pottery. For grade twelve she studied at Bethel College under the PSEO and graduated from there in 1996 with a degree in nursing.

For several years she worked in St. Mary's Hospital and married Joel Heuton in 2001. Following Joel's graduation from Mankato University, the couple joined Wycliffe, went to Indonesia, and after language school became dorm parents in Papua for the Hillcrest International School. After four years in that position and a total of five in Indonesia, they returned to Rochester to live as caregivers to her parents. Elaine home-schools their child Esther.

Craig, born in 1978, attended the Lutheran school, started high school at Lourdes and graduated from John Marshall. In these years he took an advanced math class from the University of Minnesota. He began college work at Rochester Community College, then studied geology at Iowa State University, examined the geology of Iceland by hiking around the island, and in one summer in Wyoming explored the geology in that state. After graduating from university he moved to St. Paul where he works for a company making drugs for cancer research.

Glenn, born in 1980, also attended the Lutheran school and Lourdes, played trumpet and French horn in the band, and took a pottery class, as had his sister earlier. At Bethel College he studied pottery and in January terms studied Environmental Biology in Ecuador and the Galapagos Islands. While at Bethel College he began working for Gertens, a greenhouse and landscaping company, of which he is now one of the production managers. He has a son Owen with a former girlfriend.

Paul, born in 1983, like his siblings, attended the Lutheran school and Lourdes. After graduating from high school, he attended Covenant Bible School near Calgary, Alberta, Canada, then transferred to Bethel College as an art major. During his undergraduate years he studied for one semester in Fiji under the Study Abroad Program.

While at Bethel College he was commissioned by the Department of Natural Resources to make a sculpture of a painted turtle out of junk recovered from the Mississippi River. For the same group he sculpted a huge dragonfly.

After graduation he had difficulty earning enough money as an artist. He then began to work for a builder who restored old houses. When the builder closed his business, Paul worked for two years upgrading telephone towers, but now has his own remodeling business. While in Fiji, Paul met Lizzy Hardy whom he later married. The couple now live in California with their daughter Ruth.

David and Jeannie's Parents

In 1977, when a communist government gained control of Ethiopia, the Jordans returned to the United States. For three years they worked on Bible translation from the mission house in New Wilmington, Pennsylvania, then retired to Elizabethton, Tennessee, the home of Moody Aviation. Here they did some coaching of aviators' wives on how to live in primitive places.

Jeannie's Aunt Esther moved from Illinois to be with the Jordans. Both she and Jeannie's mother suffered from dementia. When her father took the two women to dinner on Valentine's Day, both women fell and broke bones. Jeannie drove to Tennessee and brought the Jordans and Aunt Esther to Rochester where they first lived in a two-bedroom apartment in Shorewood Senior Living Campus, later in a smaller, assisted living apartment.

Mrs. Jordan died in April 2006 at the age of eighty-eight after two falls. Suffering from Parkinsonism, her husband's throat became paralyzed, and following a series of heart attacks, he died in December 2007 at the age of ninety.

By this time Kami Jordan was living with the Byers. A daughter of Jeannie's brother David, a missionary in Thailand, had been residing in Israel. But her Israeli visa had not been renewed so she came to Rochester to care for her grandparents. But when in 2006 the Jordans moved to the small, assisted living apartment, Kami joined her uncle and aunt. Jeannie comments: "We have been blessed by having Kami with us."

Everett and Adela Byer moved to Rochester in January 2008. They had gone from their farm to an apartment in the Apostolic Christian retirement home in Sabetha, Kansas. But Everett and Adela became too incapacitated to stay in their independent living apartment and no place was available in the assisted living area. David and Jeannie brought them to Rochester to the Shorewood Senior Living Campus. Everett died suddenly from heart failure in 2008. Adela was moved to a one-room apartment. She developed cancer and died in August 2009.

Here again, in overseeing the care for both sets of parents in residences near their home in Rochester, David and Jeannie acted out of their natural impulse to be of service to those in need of help.

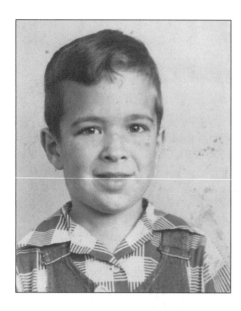

David Byer (age 3) and Jeannie Jordan (age 5). All photographs are courtesy of David and Jeannie Byer.

The Byer family. Left to right: Adela, David, Leslie, Janet, and Everett (around 1960)

The Jordan family. Back row: Jack, Chuck (Charles); front row: Dave, Mary Alice, Jeannie (1958)

Everett and Adela Byer (1995)

Charles and MaryAlice Jordan (around 1980)

Jeannie at graduation from nursing school, with her
mother, MaryAlice Jordan

Wedding party. Left to right: Phyllis Colburn,
Ann Haspels, Janet Byer, David Jordan, Francie Irwin,
Jeannie Jordan Byer, Rev. James Rhaesa, David Byer,
Bill Neely, Jack Jordan, Jim Irwin, Leslie Byer

David and Jeannie (center) with Jeannie's Sterling College
host parents, John and Lois Colburn (left) and
David's parents, Adela and Everett Byer (right)

Jeannie and David with Lois, their first child (1970)

The Byer family (1976). Left to right: Celia Byer (Leslie's wife, now deceased), Leslie Byer, Lucy Tissot (Adela's mother), Adela Byer, Janet Groff (holding Sarah Groff), Bruce Groff, Everett Byer, Jeannie Byer (holding Elaine Byer), David Byer. In front, Brian Byer and Lois Byer.

The Byer family (2001). Back row: Joe Caffrey, Lois (Byer) Caffrey, Jeannie, Brian, David, Craig. Front row: Glenn, Joel Heuton, Elaine (Byer) Heuton, Paul

Byer cousins in Kansas wheat shirts. Left to right: Glenn
Byer, Elaine Byer, Sarah Groff, Paul Byer, Lois Byer,
Eric Byer (Leslie's son), Craig Byer, Brian Byer,
Andrew Groff. (The Groffs are Janet's children.)

The Byer family at the Arctic Circle in Finland,
with their motorhome "Jaws" in the background.

David reading to children in Bulebo village (2005)

David with children in Bina Ezra's village

David with a happy baby at Macha Hospital

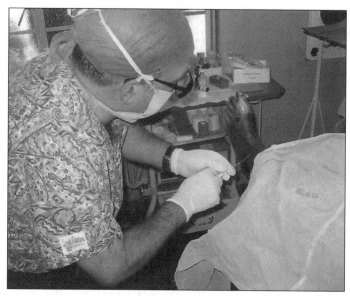

David doing an ankle block anesthesia for a toe
amputation at Macha Hospital

Examining a quilt made by Jeannie for the 80th birthday
of Bina Ezra (left). The images on the quilt are of the
Byer family, including grandchildren and Lottie and
Julian Hachaambwa and Kami Jordan

Jeannie
making
curtains
for the
Macha
nursery
school

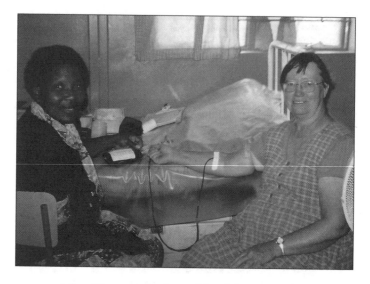

Mrs. Sikwangala draws blood from Jeannie
at Macha Hospital

Suitcases filled with medical supplies
to take to Africa.

Books brought to Zambia for the community center
near Macha

Boun Xou
Her (1989),
who lived
with the Byers
on weekends
and vacations
for four years.

Banene (Grandma) Bina Ezra

Julian (Sikalima) Haachambwa of Macha

George Greer from Poland

Kami Jordan, David and Jeannie's niece

13

The Engle Memorial Collection and Messiah College

Getting Acquainted with the College

A bright development in the lives of David and Jeannie Byer in recent years has been their warm and generous relationship with Messiah College. This relationship is reflected in gifts to the Ruth E. Engle Memorial Collection of Children's Book Illustration and in financial support of various college programs.

That this interest in Messiah College has come later in their lives may be explained in various ways. As noted, the location of the Byer family in Kansas meant that they looked to the West rather than to the East, particularly to California. David's grandmother and some great-aunts lived there, as well as other relatives. Following graduation from high school, most Kansas young people attended Upland College rather than Messiah College.

Gradually, however, Messiah College came into focus for the Byers. While at Macha, David and Jeannie met graduates of the college working in Zambia. They were impressed by the quality of these people. Messiah College, they recognized, was turning out good products.

From this initial understanding of Messiah College, the Byers came, as David put it, to realize that many of the people who were influential in his life and in the life of the Brethren in Christ were also graduates of Messiah College. In a letter to Cherie Fieser at Messiah College he wrote: "So many church leaders and friends [attended] Messiah College and we have reaped the benefit of that treasury.... I consider Messiah College an important part of my heritage."[1]

Beyond their acquaintance with Messiah College graduates in Zambia, the Byers' first direct contact with the college was through Mike Brown. David knew Mike from their Upland College days, and he and Jeannie had visited Mike in Kenya. Since that time Mike had become a librarian at Messiah College. That was additional proof to the Byers of the excellent quality of the college. When they learned that the library in 1993 had formed Friends of Murray Library and that Mike was one of the librarians responsible for its program, the Byers joined the organization as lifetime members.

Support of Friends of Murray Library

Ten years later the Byers for the first time attended the annual dinner meeting of Friends of Murray Library, attracted by the African theme of the evening. Already they had financially contributed to the Ruth E. Engle Memorial Collection of Children's Book Illustration. (A former teacher who was fond of children's books, Ruth had died the previous year.) At the dinner, the Byers were seated next to J. Harold Engle (Ruth's widower) and became better acquainted with Harold and the project. Soon they began to provide funds for the purchase of illustrations.

David and Jeannie had long been interested in children's books and the illustrations in them, an interest undoubtedly owing in part to their growing number of children. In the mid-1970s, while in London, England, they found a bookstore where the Lady Bird series could be purchased. Each book follows the same format—text on one page, an illustration on the opposite page.

They ordered approximately 350 books in the series. In 2004, David explained that "our thought was to spend money on a collection of these books rather than a *World Book Encyclopedia* which would have limited usage."[2] The Byers collected other children's books but the Lady Bird series formed the basis of the collection. "We can look at the [Lady Bird] books now," David commented, "and tell which ones were the most popular by the wear and tear on them."

The Byers also had a layperson's interest in art. In a letter in 2004 to illustrator Jim Postier (a former medical illustrator for Mayo Clinic), David admitted that neither he nor Jeannie paint nor draw. But they have been fans of Andrew Wyeth for some time, so Brandywine, Wyeth's home, "has been on our list.... At one time I was on a Rembrandt kick. I made a special trip to Munich...to the Alte Pinakothek to see their collection and to the National Gallery in London, England, to see Rembrandt's self-portraits."[3]

In the same letter he referred to the "eclectic display" of art in their living room. It includes an oil painting of the traditional Ethiopian story of the Queen of Sheba and King Solomon, a watercolor by Jane Destro of an Asian and a Caucasian girl hugging each other, an oil painting of a scene in Thailand, and a watercolor of the Byer house painted by their friend Dr. Peter Southorn. Two icons, one of Christ the Good Shepherd in the Egyptian Coptic style and another of the baptism of Christ in the Russian Orthodox style, are periodically alternated on a wall. A chalk drawing by Helen Sviderskis also graces a living room wall. "That one," David recalled, "she painted the day after I visited Helen and her husband in New York. It is of the bouquet of flowers I had presented to them the previous evening."

To their grandchildren David and Jeannie gave original children's book illustrations, together with signed copies of the books in which they appear. They made their gifts as follows: to Vanessa (daughter of Lois and Joe) an illustration by David McPhail from Eugene Field's *Wynken, Blynken, and Nod*; to Owen (son of Glenn) an illustration by Julia Cairns from Laurie Krebs's *We All Went on Safari*; to Joshua, Grant, and Nathan (sons of Brian and Sharon) an illustration by Chris Wormell from his book *Ferocious Wild Beasts!*; to Esther (daughter of Elaine and Joel) an illustration from *Two Frogs*, also written and illustrated by Chris Wormell; to Ruth (daughter of Paul and Lizzy) an illustration from *Building Our House*, written and illustrated by Jonathan Bean. To Sharon's mother, of Irish descent, they gave a copy of a book of Irish tales and an illustration by David McPhail.

While having an interest in art, the Byers realized that if they were to sponsor the purchase of artwork for the Engle Collection, they needed to become more knowledgeable about children's books and the illustrations they contain. To this end David became a Friend of the Kerlan Collection at the University of Minnesota in Minneapolis. The Kerlan Collection has one of the world's largest children's literature collections. Included in the collection are more than 90,000 children's books, primarily by twentieth-century American writers, as well as manuscripts and illustration material for over 10,000 additional titles. Also in the collection are over 300 periodical titles, as well as letters, posters, toys, photographs and audiovisuals.[4]

There was obviously much in the Kerlan Collection to educate the Byers in children's literature and illustrations. But more than this, David volunteered to assist in digitizing the Collection's finding aids. He chose the letter L to digitize, so that in the process of this work he entered such well-known writers and artists as Madeleine L'Engle, E. B. Lewis, Dorothy Lathrop, and Lois Lowry.

He clearly enjoyed this volunteer work. He periodically drove the eighty-five miles to the Kerlan Collection, getting out of bed early in the morning to spend the day on a computer. He liked working under the direction of Karen Nelson Hoyle whom he described as "a delightful person and a very capable individual."

He also increased his knowledge of art and children's books by attending lectures and conferences on the subject. The first of these conferences was the 34th Annual Festival for Young People at the University of Iowa in October 2004. The next year he went to the Children's Africana Book Awards in Washington, D. C., also attended, at David's suggestion, by four members of the Friends of Murray Library selection committee which chooses illustrations for the Engle Memorial Collection. The following year he attended a lecture by Linnea Christensen who was serving on the Caldecott Award Committee. In her presentation she discussed what the committee looks for, including inconsistencies, when they judge art in children's books.[5]

At these and later conferences and lectures David sometimes posed questions to the speaker. At the Iowa conference he asked E. B. Lewis, one of the speakers, whether artists ever suffer from the equivalent of "writers' block." Lewis replied that instead of blockage he likes to think of progress; his work is always in progress. Similarly he talked with other specialists in the field. At an international conference, he conversed with the Curator-at-Large for the collection of children's book illustrations at the Israel Museum in Jerusalem and from him received the interesting information that the museum's children's books are arranged in order of illustrator, not author.

At first the Byers' contributions to the Engle Memorial Collection were monetary. Soon, however, they became involved in helping to locate and suggest illustrations.

Their involvement was very active. David made a determined effort to locate illustrations. He used libraries and special collections, such as the Kerlan and the nearby Rochester Public Library, which contained an excellent selection of children's books. He reviewed lists of award-winning illustrators, made internet searches, and visited galleries specializing in the sale of original book illustrations, such as one in California (where they found Chris Raschka's illustration for *The Hello, Goodbye Window*), John Huddy's Illustration Cupboard in London, England, and a children's bookstore in southern Minneapolis. He regularly searched publication lists produced by Barnes & Noble and Amazon.com.

When finding a likely addition to the Engle Memorial Collection, the Byers informed Cherie Fieser at Messiah College of their discovery. David's letters to Cherie contain many examples of such action. In May 2007, for example, he went online after reading *Sundiata: Lion King of Mali* and came across a discussion of David Wisniewski's *Golem*. He liked the illustrations (for the Golem), so he searched online and found Wisniewski's illustrations available for sale. He thought the selection committee might be interested in purchasing one of the illustrations.[6] The selection committee was interested but the cost was prohibitive. The Byers agreed and negotiations ended.

Another example of the Byers' involvement with the Engle Memorial Collection was drawing attention to the work of Baba Wagué Diakité. As reported in the Rochester Library's Electronic Newsletter, the Byers read *The Magic Gourd*, written and illustrated by Diakité. This book suggested a fulfillment of a dream of the Byer family to include in the Engle Memorial Collection the work of an African-born illustrator (Diakité was born in Timbuktu, Mali, but lives in the United States).[7] One illustration is a 21-inch chameleon sculpture, another a ceramic bowl which appears to be full of insects. The author-illustrator had received a Children's Africana Book Award in 2004. David read about the award and found the book in the Rochester Public Library. The Byers contacted Cherie Fieser and expressed their willingness to sponsor the purchase of artwork by Diakité for the Engle Memorial Collection. The selection committee was able to purchase not only the chameleon and ceramic bowl but also a ceramic tile illustration that Diakité created for *The Pot of Wisdom*.

Still another example of the Byers' involvement with the Engle Memorial Collection is David's question to Cherie about whether the selection committee was pursuing Roberto Innocenti illustrations. "That would be great, especially as he now receives the 2008 Hans Christian Andersen Award for illustration. How much money is needed for an Innocenti?"[8] Cherie had already begun negotiations with a gallery to secure an illustration from Innocenti's *Pinocchio*.

When David and Jeannie visited the Brandywine Museum in June 2004, they saw *Goose Moon*, a book illustrated by Jim Postier, prominently displayed at the entrance to the museum shop with some toy stuffed geese. David thought he should tell Postier of their visit; he informed the author-artist that, although many other books were for sale, the shop was obviously promoting *Goose Moon* at that time. David's contact with Postier paved the way for a book signing at the Brandywine.

David apprised Cherie of his and Postier's numerous email exchanges because he thought the selection committee might be interested in some of Postier's original artwork. He sent Postier a portfolio of the Engle Memorial Collection and encouraged him to visit Messiah College and "look up the Fiesers."

Cherie presented to the selection committee the possibility of acquiring a piece of Postier's work. However, the consensus of the committee was that "we should focus on other styles and media right now, since ours is still a fledgling collection." This interchange was in August 2004, only five months after the dedication of the Collection. Clearly, the Byers were already vigorously following their interest in and support of the Engle Memorial Collection.

Several informal understandings guided the Byers and those responsible for the Engle Memorial Collection. The Byers were free to suggest illustrations, but the selection committee makes the final decision on whether to obtain an illustration. Some of the Byers' suggestions were not accepted. Conversely, the selection committee could make suggestions to the Byers if it had funds remaining from what the Byers had earlier sent. In this latter understanding, the Byers were very generous in accepting the committee's recommendations. They were also free to dedicate each artwork to a person or persons of their choice. (For more on the illustrations, see appendices III and IV containing photographs of the Byers' donations and Cherie Fieser's account of their acquisition.)

In a presentation at the annual dinner meeting of Friends of Murray Library in 2005, David described the manner in which they arrived at obtaining their first donated illustration. "Our starting point was with children's book author Jane Kurtz whom we have known for many years. Shortly after the 1994 publication of *Fire on the Mountain*, Jane gave us an inscribed copy. Her books have drawn the attention of a number of award committees. We thought she should be represented in the Engle Collection. E. B. Lewis illustrates three of her books [including *Fire on the Mountain*].… We didn't find any illustrations from [these books], but we liked Lewis's work.

"This led to E. B. Lewis's illustration 'Bessie at the Window,' from Nikki Grimes's book *Talkin' about Bessie: The Story of Aviator Bessie Coleman.* This title was named the 2003 Coretta Scott King Illustrator Award winner, and was also a 2003 Coretta Scott King Author Honor book. We sponsored it in honor of Lydia Byer and Mary E. Byer."

Other Gifts to Messiah College

Even before attending their first Friends of Murray Library annual meeting in 2003, the Byers had been on the college campus. Their visits to the college began with attending one of the college's annual Christmas dinners, conveniently occurring when David was in Pennsylvania to attend a board meeting of the Macha Malaria Research Institute.

Their "adopted" daughter Julian and her husband, Dr. Lottie Hachaambwa from Zambia, were with the Byers at this Christmas dinner. A daughter and niece of Jon Stuckey (of the college's development office) and his wife Shari cared for the Hachaambwa baby during the dinner and program. The Byers were impressed by this kindness of a college administrator and his family, as they were by the dinner. "It was such a blessing," David later commented, "to hear a truly Christian presentation of the meaning of Christmas." He spoke similarly of a later college Christmas dinner that he and Jeannie attended: "As I told some here in Rochester, I felt so blessed that I felt like shouting Hallelujah, but I didn't think it was a Hallelujah crowd, and I didn't want to be disrespectful. Two families at our table are retired faculty who are in the process of endowing scholarships. This was a big encouragement to us [to trust in the college and to make donations]."

Following their first college Christmas dinner, the Byers proceeded to make substantial financial gifts to the college. Understandably, they endowed a scholarship in their names for international students, and donated money to the Direct Aid and Emergency Fund, also for students from abroad. They contributed to the endowment of the Roy and Dorothy Sider Missionary Debt Foregiveness Fund which pays the college debt of students who go into missionary service, because, as David said, "We do not like indebtedness, especially when it is creating a barrier to missionary service." And they assisted in endowing the E. Morris and D. Leone Sider Institute for Anabaptist, Pietist, and Wesleyan Studies.

They also made both monetary and artifact donations to the archives of Messiah College and the Brethren in Christ Church. The monetary donation was for converting old tapes to a digital format. The artifact was a cottage cheese container from the Belle Springs creamery in

Kansas. David explained, "We were interested in the Belle Springs creamery that was operated by Brethren in Christ settlers around Abilene, Kansas...because it was a successful adventure by Brethren in Christ to create a cash flow in the midst of farming disasters, such as drought."

The Byers made all of these donations without being solicited, with the small exception of one instance when the college presented a special student need.

Jon Stuckey has described David and Jeannie Byer as "good ambassadors for the college. They even have a college sticker on a window in one of their cars. Their attitude about the college is always positive. They promote the college in an affirmative way. They are a lovely couple—simple lifestyle, gracious, welcoming, Christlike, reflecting the gospel."

In these words, Jon, in effect, reminds the reader of the many opportunities for service that David and Jeannie welcomed, and of their encouragement, by their words and deeds, to "live simply and give generously."

14

Postscript

For David and Jeannie, the year 2014 was a mixture of enjoyment, health problems, and death. In January, both were sufficiently healthy to travel to California to visit son Paul and his family, as well as Byer and Tissot aunts, uncles, and cousins.

Later, although not responding well to chemotherapy for myeloma, David was given a four-week break from treatments. He and Jeannie used these weeks to visit friends David and Diane Tuck in England and friends in Zambia. Special to them was their visit with "Granny" Bina Ezra in her village of Bulebo, and with their "daughter" Julian, her husband Lottie and their two daughters, Tite and Lumba.

By the time of their return to Rochester, David felt very weak. A bone marrow biopsy revealed that his marrow count was 90 percent involved with myeloma. In April he was hospitalized for six days during which time he received intensive chemotherapy.

Myeloma continued to return every few weeks despite new chemotherapy treatments. But he thought he was sufficiently well to fly to Pennsylvania in early October to attend the annual dinner meeting of the Brethren in Christ Historical Society and to visit friends in the area. But by the time he returned to Rochester he was feeling very ill. Elaine met him at the airport and took him directly to the emergency room. Later he was in and out of the hospital every few days.

But his myeloma could not be controlled. After two weeks in the intensive care unit, all his systems failed. He died on November 7. At his request his body was donated to Mayo Clinic, with burial later in the Pleasant Hill cemetery in Kansas, on the site of the church of his childhood and youth. Jeannie describes the celebration of his life on December 16 as "a wonderful worship service that followed his wishes."

Meanwhile, Jeannie also had severe health problems. At the end of January, she received steroid injections for her arthritis and pinched nerves, but they gave her only temporary relief. The unrelenting pain led to depression and to her wish to die. An operation for fusion of sacroiliac joints was recommended, but at the surgeon's office she had what she calls a "meltdown" upon learning that the operation would involve general anesthesia (two earlier operations on her spine using general anesthetic had caused her much misery). Considered suicidal, she was put on a seventy-two-hour psychiatric hold.

David resolved this impasse by contacting an anesthesiologist who assured the Byers that she could administer general anesthesia without pain. With this assurance and the prospect of relief from her suffering, Jeannie's will to live returned. She had successful surgery on October 9, although pain in her left leg and right S-1 joint still troubles her.

She continues to live in the same house that she and David shared for many years, along with daughter Elaine, Joel, the couple's daughter Esther, and her niece Kami.

Endnotes

Chapter 1

[1] Mennonites belong to one of the descendant groups of the original Anabaptists.

[2] For the experiences of Mennonites and other peace groups during the Revolutionary War, see Richard K. McMaster, *Land, Piety, Peoplehood: The Establishment of Mennonite Communities in America, 1683-1790* (Scottdale, PA: Herald Press, 1985), chapter 10.

[3] This historical background to the Byer family was compiled by Everett Byer and David Byer. Everett Byer's research materials are in the Brethren in Christ Archives at Messiah College in Grantham, Pennsylvania. Part of David's research may be found in email letters to family members. These letters are in the family's possession.

[4] For the movement of Brethren in Christ to Kansas in these years, see Carlton O. Wittlinger, *Quest for Piety and Obedience: The Story of the Brethren in Christ* (Nappanee, IN: Evangel Press, 1978), pp. 132, 146-148. The movement is also covered by Wilma J. Musser in "Brethren in Christ Churches in Kansas: A Historical Survey," *Brethren in Christ History and Life* (August 1991), pp. 135-155.

[5] *Evangelical Visitor*, November 11, 1935, p. 8.

[6] For her obituary, see ibid., March 25, 1970, p. 15.

[7] Adela and Everett's photos with captions are in the same yearbook (*The Echo*) of 1934, and on the same page (p. 7).

[8] The historical background of Jeannie's ancestors and family may be found in a presentation to a Sunday school class of the Salem Road Covenant Church, Rochester, Minnesota in the fall of 2013. David also made a similar presentation. Both are in the possession of the Byers.

Chapter 2

[1] Much of the information on David's childhood is from his sister, Janet Byer Groff, letter to author, June 20, 2014.

[2] David Byer, interview, June 2014. Unless otherwise designated, the text throughout the book comes from interviews or emails from David or Jeannie Byer.

[3] *The Hornet Yearbook, 1960.*

[4] David Byer to Hamlin high school class reunion, May 20, 2010.

[5] Leslie Byer, letter to author, July 12, 2014.

[6] *St. Joseph Gazette* (n.d.) (in Everett Byer's papers).

[7] Austin and Rhoda Heise, email to author, April 29, 2014.

[8] *Evangelical Visitor*, October 10, 1982, p. 15.

[9] For the history of the Kansas youth camp, see Bonnie Frey, "Camp Is Wonderful: Everybody Friendly": The Kansas Youth Camp, *Brethren in Christ History and Life* (August 2009), pp. 284-307.

Chapter 3

[1] As with David's information in the previous chapter and later in the text, information supplied by Jeannie will not be documented unless there is a special need to do so.

[2] Jeannie has written the following description of this eye disease: "A very common disease in Africa is trachoma, an infection of the eye lids. It causes scarring, which draws the eyelashes in toward the eyeball. When the person blinks, the eyelashes rub on the cornea. After antibiotic ointment treatment to heal the infection, surgery can be done to release the scar to allow the lashes to turn outward, away from the cornea. An incision is made along the lash line on the inside. An almond-shaped section of skin is removed from the outer eyelid. When the edges are sutured together, the lashes are drawn outward and away from the cornea. My mother was taught to do this procedure and did several thousand of them in Sudan and Ethiopia. She even taught several doctors to do the procedure."

[3] David Jordan, email to author, July 10, 2014.

Chapter 4

[1] Phyllis (Colburn) Tucker, letter to author, June 29, 2014.

[2] Adela Byer to family, December 28, 1966. The marriage is reported in the *Evangelical Visitor*, January 16, 1967, p. 22.

Chapter 5

[1] Peter Southorn, email to author, July 5, 2014.

[2] Steven R. Rettke, email to author, July 10, 2014.

[3] Ibid.

[4] Southorn, email.

[5] Rettke, email.

Chapter 6

[1] David to parents, April 7, 1967.

[2] David to parents, April 9, 1967.

3 David to Janet Byer, April 7, 1967.

4 David to parents, April 7, 1967.

5 David to Janet, April 7, 1967.

6 David to parents, April 9, 1967.

7 David to parents, May 20, 1967.

8 Mike Brown to Morris Sider, letter of June 30, 2014.

Chapter 7

1 David to parents, no date.

2 For a biography of Frances Davidson, see E. Morris Sider, *Nine Portraits: Brethren in Christ Biographical Sketches* (Nappanee, IN: Evangel Press, 1978), pp. 157-212. The early history of Brethren in Christ missions is covered by Carlton O. Wittlinger, *Quest for Piety and Obedience*, chapter IX.

3 In 2006 the hospital contained 208 beds. It was a referral center for an estimated population of from 70,000 to 100,000.

4 David to parents, December 21, 1968; January 6, 1969; August 3, 1969.

5 David to parents, December 21, 1968.

6 David to parents, March 24, 1969; July 20, 1969.

7 David to parents (no date), 1970.

8 *Evangelical Visitor*, April 10, 1971, p. 14.

9 David to parents, December 21, 1968; January 2, 1969.

10 David to parents, July 29, 1968.

11 David to parents, March 30, 1969.

12 David to parents, June 23, 1969.

13 David to parents, June 1, 1970.

14 David to parents, February 6, 1969.

15 David to parents, August 3, 1969.

16 David to parents, April 2, 1969.

[17] David to parents, July 20, 1969.

[18] David to parents, August 30, 1969.

[19] Jeannie to the Byers, attached to David's letter of August 30, 1969.

Chapter 8

[1] Jeannie in David's letter to parents, March 11, 1969.

[2] David to parents, June 10, 1969.

[3] David to parents, September 13, 1969.

[4] Ibid.

[5] Jeannie to David's parents, June, 1969.

[6] David to parents, October 30, 1969.

[7] David to parents, June 15, 1969.

[8] David to parents, June 23, 1969.

[9] David to parents, September 14 and October 30, 1969.

[10] John and Esther Spurrier, email to author, June 15, 2014.

[11] David to parents, January 6, 1969.

[12] David to parents, May 18, 1970.

[13] David to parents, July 20, 1969.

[14] David to parents, February 6, 1969.

[15] David to parents, August 3, 1969.

[16] David to parents, January 6, 1969.

[17] David to parents, March 4, 1970.

[18] David to parents, August 3, 1969.

[19] David to parents, September 14, 1969.

Chapter 9

[1] Esther Spurrier, email.

[2] Paul Byer, email to author, July 13, 2014.

[3] Jeannie Byer, newsletter, New Year, 2011.

[4] Paul Byer, email.

[5] Samuel Brubaker, email to author, November 17, 2014.

[6] Jeannie Byer, presentation to Salem Road Sunday school, September 16, 2102.

[7] Arlene Schuiteman, email to author, July 3, 2014.

[8] *Sioux Center News,* April 9, 2012.

[9] *Mayo Anesthesia Newsletter,* May 2005, p. 9.

[10] Jeannie gives credit to other Africans for influencing them spiritually. "When Arthur Kutshwayo prayed, you could tell that he was ignoring all the people around him and was speaking directly to God. [As David noted] Rev. and Mrs. Joseph Sikalima were wonderful examples of hospitality and generosity, Rev. Sampson Mudenda taught us how the strong influence of witchcraft made it difficult for African Christians to believe in the power of God. Bina Ezra taught us by example about praying constantly and the joy of singing hymns."

Chapter 10

[1] David Byer, letter to the editor, *Post Bulletin,* October 28, 2006.

[2] Mark Evinger, email to author, July 9, 2014.

[3] Dawn Schuett, "Booklet Sheds Light on Neighborly Laws," October 13, 1998.

[4] David, email to author, May 27, 2014.

[5] David to parents, August 6, 1984.

Chapter 11

[1] Eugene Hokanson, email to author, July 5, 2014

[2] Mark Evinger, email to author, July 9, 2014.

[3] Devotion for Friday, November 22, 1985.

[4] Steve and Arlene Burgert, email to author, June 23, 2014.

5 Mark Evinger, email to David Byer, April 15, 2014.

6 Ron and Sheryl Peterson, email to author, June 22, 2014.

7 Paul Byer, email to author, July 13, 2014.

8 Jeannie Byer, "Following Jesus: Missions," presentation to Salem Road Church, September 16, 2012.

9 Ibid.

10 David, email to Cherie Fieser, July 1, 2008.

11 Devotion for November 18, 1985.

12 Letter to the editor, *Pioneer Press*, January 2, 2003.

13 David to parents, May 19, 1986. The letter contains the information on his visit to Orthodox and Episcopalian services.

14 Devotion for November 18, 1985.

15 David to parents, October 23, 1976.

16 Devotional for November 23, 1985.

17 David to Valerie Rempel, September 3, 2014.

Chapter 12

1 Lois Byer Caffrey, letter to author, June 15, 2014.

2 Eugene Hokanson, email to author, July 5, 2014.

3 Leslie Byer, email to author, July 7, 2014.

4 Caffrey letter.

5 The wide range of countries from which guests came is commented on in *Mayo Anesthesiologist Alumni Newsletter,* May 2005, Vol. 4, No. 8.

6 David to Hamlin High School reunion, May 20, 2010.

7 Presentation to Salem Road Church, September 2012.

8 David to parents, May 19, 1986.

9 David to parents, August 6, 1984.

10 David Byer, "Parents Deserve Better," letter to editor, *Post Bulletin*, May 26, 2005.

[11] David to parents, August 6, 1984.

[12] For a genealogical trip, see David to family, November 15, 1977; for trip to Pennsylvania, see November 15, 1979.

[13] Information on the Byer children was provided by their mother in an email to author, November 22, 2014.

Chapter 13

[1] David to Cherie Fieser, May 9, 2010. Cherie is Library Special Projects Administrator and Curator of Book Arts, including Curator of the Ruth E. Engle Memorial Collection of Children's Book Illustration.

[2] David to Fieser, September 6, 2004.

[3] David to Jim Postier, September 1, 2004.

[4] Kerlan Friends, description of resources, University of Minnesota.

[5] David to Cherie, May 4, 2006.

[6] David to Cherie, May 12, 2007.

[7] Rochester Public Library Electronic Newsletter, November 2008, Vol. 23, No. 11.

[8] David to Cherie, July 1, 2008.

Appendices

Appendix I

A Family Trip Through Europe

by Jeannie Byer

After about 7,200 air miles, 7,058 road miles, 500 train and ferry miles, approximately 880 gallons of gasoline, eight currencies, six languages, twenty maps and several thousand searches for *large* parking spaces, the Byer family is back in Rochester.

About a year and a half ago, while visiting Quebec City, we were challenged with the idea of touring Europe with all eight family members. We had been there before as a couple and with various combinations of two or three children but never with all six kids.

Elaine and I took our motorhome to Baltimore the middle of May to be shipped, and we flew back to Rochester. The whole family left on Memorial Day to pick up the motorhome in Liverpool, England.

We had never visited Liverpool, so we enjoyed our two days there visiting the cathedral, the Maritime Museum, and Liverpool Museum. Interesting taste experiences were the hotel's large salty, bony, breakfast kippers and take-out pizza with sweet corn and artichokes on it. Keeping on the left side of the road was a nerve-racking experience, especially when we were trying to enter a round-about (traffic circle) with the bulk of the motorhome blocking our view from the left-hand driver seat.

Because the kids wanted to go to Scotland, we drove to the city of Edinburgh which was a favorite from other trips. We had the first experience of trying to find a whale-sized parking spot when the city was equipped for minnows. After visiting the castle, a park with a telescope-shaped monument to Nelson, and climbing up a huge hill named Arthur's seat, we headed south along the seacoast till we came to the causeway to the island of Lindesfarne. The island with a castle and ruined priory was very peaceful except for the bleating of sheep.

In Warwickshire we renewed our friendship with the Tarlow family who had moved into Homestead Village on the same snowy winter day in 1970 as we had. While head-quartered at their home, we visited Warwick Castle again, Ironbridge Open-air Museum of the Industrial Revolution, Coalport Pottery Museum, and Stratford-on-Avon.

Heading south from the Birmingham area we parked at the vicarage in Pinner, a northwestern suburb of London. The David Tuck family were our neighbors when we lived in Zambia and it was wonderful to see them again. The vicarage was only a five-minute walk from the train station where we began our commutes to the sights of London.

Old favorites in London were St. Paul's Cathedral, Madame Tussaud's Waxworks, and the Tower of London. This time we also sampled the shopping area of Covent Garden, the London Transport Museum, and Hamely's (an enormous toy store). We had never been in the south of England so we toured Winchester and Salisbury Cathedrals, Stonehenge, and Old Sarum. Craig, the historian in our family, scampered eagerly around the battlefield near Hastings where William, invading from France, had earned the title "the Conqueror."

We took the Sealink ferry from Dover to Calais, France. It was a big relief to drive on the right side of the road again but difficult to decipher signs since none of us knew French.

In the small town of Bayeaux we tried our first crêpes and visited the marvelous tapestry telling the story of the battle of Hastings. Later we went to the WW II invasion site and cemetery at Utah Beach before we headed to Mont St. Michel. After touring the Abbey the next day we headed for Chartres Cathedral with the most beautiful stained glass windows. In the campground that evening we must have interrupted some kind of clan gathering because there were people frowning, yelling and gesticulating at us. After we pulled over to the wash building to fill our tank with water, we parked near the tents and slept with easier minds.

In the Versailles campground we parked next to a camper van with a German tag and a family playing badminton. When Paul returned their shuttlecock, the man said, "Merci" to him and Paul said to us, "That man taught me French." It turned out that the family was American from Alaska and "merci" was one of the few words of French they knew.

Dave packed his bag and brief case for the flight back to Rochester. The train station was near the campground, making it easy for us to get to Paris the next day. Dave went on to the airport to return to his work at Mayo Clinic and the rest of us went up the Eiffel Tower and took a boat tour on the Seine River. We had our map out to locate all the sights so we could find them again later. The kids began their education in the art of buying ice cream in different languages and currencies. Everyone and all the tour books said *never* to drive in Paris but we decided to try it anyway.

We left the Versailles campground early Sunday morning and only got lost once on the way to Paris. The roads and streets were completely empty so we were able to drive slowly around the Arc de Triomphe, Place de la Concorde, Notre Dame Cathedral, Tuileries Garden, and the Louvre before traffic started to get thick and we headed east toward Rheims.

We compared David Macaulay's book *Cathedral* to the architecture of the one in Rheims, imagining all the time and effort it took to build it. Lois asked some German tourists where they got the tarts they were eating and they directed us to a bakery where we loaded up on pastries and bread. We phoned our friends, the Litchinkos, in Nancy and they said they had a good spot for us to park. They gave us a wonderful tour of this very interesting city. We enjoyed the Historical Museum and Stanislas Place, the city square with golden gates and wonderful fountains at each corner. While eating at an elegant restaurant, we enjoyed the sound and light show where the statue of Count Stanislas, associated with the French Revolution, seems to come to life. The Daum Crystallerie was a fascinating place where we watched exquisite vases being made by expert glass blowers.

On the road from Nancy to Strasbourg are the towns of Luneville and St. Clement, famous for faience pottery. We were really enjoying the cathedral and other picturesque buildings in Strasbourg until we were trying to leave and made a wrong turn into the old city. The lane was extremely narrow, the low second stories jutted out over the street. Our van was too long to make it around a corner and there were about twenty cars behind us honking and the drivers were shouting things we were glad we couldn't understand. While I sat in panic in the driver's seat, near tears, wishing we had never left Rochester, and praying we wouldn't have to reverse for five or six blocks, Brian kept his head, walked ahead a block and said he thought we could make it through to where the street widened. When we made it through that harrowing experience, we stopped with relief at an ice cream stand and relaxed for quite a while before continuing on to Karlsruhe.

When we entered Switzerland we paid a road tax to use the major highways. On the receipt we were classified as a bus, which in some places allowed us to park in the bus zones. The Basel zoo was as good as the recommendations we had read. Driving from Basel to Neuchatel was *awesome*. The road was narrow and wound around the base of immense mountains and beside sparkling streams.

By this time we were used to being ogled but at Columbier we were really surprised when we pulled in and lots of campers left their dinner tables and came out to stare. Some of our ancestors had come from Valengin to Nebraska. We explored the church and castle in the small town on Sunday afternoon. After seeing the family coat of arms in the church's stained glass windows, we enjoyed the monthly lace-making demonstration at the castle.

In Geneva we were allowed to use the tour bus parking area when we went to the dock for a boat tour of the lake. When we were on the way to the cathedral we saw archaeologists digging up bones with trowels and brushes. The weather grew worse so we couldn't visit Lausanne. All through Switzerland we kept thinking, "Surely this must be the most beautiful spot on earth"—until we found another spot and it was even better! Berne was another favorite place. The bear pit with the agile cubs, the clock tower, and the amusing fountains were intriguing.

We found that Switzerland has a family card for train travel which lets children under 16 travel free. We wanted to see the Matterhorn but I was afraid to drive on the roads through the mountains with a terrific drop off the side, so we drove on to a lovely campground near the train station in Frutigen. A ten-minute walk from the campground brought us to the train station where we began a day of incredible views as we traveled by train to Zermatt, hoping to see the Matterhorn. I was so happy to be riding instead of driving as we passed the road several times and saw it perched high above the deep valleys. It was drizzling in Zermatt so we couldn't see much. Brian, Craig and Glenn rode the cable car to Schwartzsee to get closer to the Matterhorn. It was even rainier and very cold but they did get a few glimpses. Lois, Elaine, Paul, and I went to a restaurant for hot chocolate while waiting for the boys to return.

We made it to a campground by the lake in Zurich. The kids had been asking what we were going to do on July 4th, but we were able to celebrate a couple of days early. Zurich was having a festival with an airshow and fireworks over the lake in the evening. We had planned a walking tour of Zurich but were rained out and exhausted from being kept awake to the wee small hours by boisterous neighbors. Later in the day we had a gorgeous view of Lake Constance when the sun broke through. It was quite an experience to go through a mountain in a ten-mile-long tunnel just after entering Austria.

We stopped at a quiet rest area for dinner and decided to stay for the night. In the morning we held a vote and decided to visit the northern town of Bolzano, Italy, for some real pizza. Trying to visit the city of Bolzano brought back the nightmare of Strasbourg as we kept coming to arches over the road which seemed to get progressively smaller. We gave up and started to return to the highway, stopping at a hotel/restaurant advertising pizza. Unfortunately it was after 2 p.m. when the restaurant closes till 9 p.m. We settled for ham sandwiches, ice cream, and chocolate bars before heading back to Innsbruck and a campground by the river.

Driving around the next day, we found no place to park. When we tried the bus parking place, the attendant came at our windshield with a big stick so we made a hasty exit and headed toward Salzburg over a country road. There was a very hot wind blowing and we couldn't get either of the air conditioners to work. The thermometer in the motorhome said 98°F and outside was 34°C. It was time to choose luxury over economy; we found a wonderful campground with lots of shade and a swimming pool.

We left the motorhome and took the minibus to the city center where we had an interesting day visiting Mirabel Palace, the Mozart house, and the Hohensalzburg Castle, which we reached by a funicular railway. From the castle we could watch men in the square below playing chess with giant playing pieces and could see musicians performing with their instrument cases out to collect tips and donations. The little kids said that Brian and Elaine should practice the trumpet and flute at Silver Lake and see if they could make any money.

Brian found the Castle Hochsterwitz pictured in the *Castles of Europe* and said it looked like we could get there even though the road looked tiny on the map. After parking at the base of the hill, we walked up the spiral road to the castle, going through the different deterrents to invasion.

We stayed on the Autobahn and parked near the Yugoslavia border at another rest area for the night.

When we got to Vienna, we were delighted with the broad streets and avenues. There seemed to be plenty of parking and we found a spot in front of the Opera House. After stringing the inside of the motorhome with drying laundry, we set out on foot to tour the downtown area. I had an interesting chat with an elderly gentleman on a park bench by the statue of Mozart. He spoke German and I spoke English but we were able to understand each other and enjoyed the conversation. We walked through the huge courtyard and toured the imperial palace, imagining what it would be like to live in such an elegant place. The tree-shaded walk along the boulevard was refreshing.

Back at the motorhome for a cold drink and some ice cream, we saw people lining up for an opera house tour so we hurried on over. What a beautiful building! The sets from "Aida" were back stage and we could imagine what it would be like to attend that opera in those gorgeous surroundings.

Driving past Salzburg the next day, we heard a flopping noise and discovered one hubcap was missing and an inside rear tire was flat. We crept along to the first exit and enquired at the military barrier at the base of the exit ramp where we could get the tire fixed. The soldiers directed us to a service station where the manager decided we were too big and led us to another garage. They used three jacks to get the wheel up high enough to change the shredded inner tube.

On the way again we headed for Munich and the Deutches Museum. We spent only two hours there before closing time and the kids wanted to see more. At dusk we strolled around the campground where we had parked and saw the enormous fifth wheel vehicle owned by an American with side rooms extended and three axles at the back. We were disgusted at the campground's sinks full of old spaghetti and other debris, and glad we were self-contained.

The next day we headed for Dachau. At the site of the concentration camp we were all saddened and horrified at the way some humans had treated others. Our five-year-old Paul went through the picture exhibit clinging to my leg and asking, "Why were these people so bad to the other people?" Bigotry and hate are difficult to explain to someone who has experienced only love. We went back to our peaceful campsite by the lake but everyone had bad dreams that night.

The fairy tale castle at Neuschwanstein was another old favorite. This time we rode up the easy way in a horse carriage instead of trudging up the narrow zig-zag path we had gone up last time, pushing two little guys in the buggy. We couldn't imagine living there but it was fantastic to visit. The next morning we did a thorough housecleaning and tanked up with water before going back to Hohen-schwangau. It was very homey for a castle and we could imagine living there.

Glenn had been feeling sick for a couple of days with a fever and bad cold so we were glad to stop, relax, and enjoy the friendship and hospitality of friends in Heidenheim. Wolfgang and Maxi Breuninger and son Martin were such good hosts when we were there eight years before and we had enjoyed visits from their sons Bernie and Andy in Rochester. Martin took the boys for a haircut and I took the motorhome for an oil change. I forgot to take an interpreter but by sign language we got the job done. Back at Breuningers we managed to fit most of the motorhome in their driveway by parking diagonally. We visited an ancient seashore, the local castle which houses an interesting coach and sleigh museum, a Roman bath with water from hot mineral springs, and a shopping area.

On Sunday Maxi and her visiting schoolmate, Inge, translated for us when we went with them to their local church. The pastor spoke on building bridges between men and God and between peoples. He showed bridge slides to illustrate different points, one of which was the Europa Bridge which we had just crossed a few days before. When we met after the service, he apologized for not having a picture of the Golden Gate Bridge.

The next morning was a festival day in Ulm where Bernie Breuninger lives. After some of the kids climbed the highest cathedral spire in the world, we walked through the ancient fisherman's village to the edge of the Danube River for a boat parade. It was a glorious sunny afternoon which had everyone in high spirits. We joined the crowd making its way along the river to the park where more festivities were in progress. Bernie met us by the aquarium and took us on several rides similar to the county fair rides here. We went in search of food and drink. I do not know what we consumed but we enjoyed the food and fun immensely before cramming all seven of us into Bernie's Volkswagen for the ride home.

We interrupted our drive to Hanover the next day to empty our holding tanks, and fill our water tanks. Lois cut my hair while we did a couple of loads of laundry as our wash water was going out the drain. When we got near Hanover, we called Horst and Marge Hohenhaus to let them know we were on the way. Marge had been my teacher in high school and we had a good time chatting about old times. We visited Vogelpark, a sort of zoo for endangered birds. The little kids had a marvelous time at the Kinderparadist playground. The splendid birds were complemented by beautiful flowers and shrubbery.

From Wunsdorf we made a quick drive to Amsterdam and found a lovely campground near the airport so the next morning we could meet Dave who was rejoining us. We collected Dave, now returned from Rochester, and spent an interesting afternoon touring a windmill and the ethnic museum, and enjoying wonderful pastries. We spent the evening with our friend Solko Schalm in Rotterdam. At the time we didn't realize that it is illegal to park recreational vehicles on the street or that the attorney general for Holland lives across the road.

Saturday morning Solko brought us an armload of warm bread fresh from the bakery. At his recommendation we visited the Delta Expo where the storm-surge barrier project is exhibited. The engineering of that project was incredible with the design of huge piers, gates, base mats and four enormous ships especially designed to build the system.

During lunch in the motorhome, a man came up and asked if we were Americans. When we said yes, he asked how many of us there were. He handed eight large gold stars in the door. A short while later, while we were stopped for gas, the same man pulled up behind us and came over to explain that his father had been liberated from the Dachau concentration camp by American soldiers and his family was very grateful.

We camped in Antwerp, Belgium. In the morning the campground manager gave us a city map and called the diamond museum to find out where it was and what time it was open. We found a place to park with the tour busses behind the railway station. When we walked to the diamond museum, we found that it wasn't there anymore but was moving and wouldn't open again till October. Both the miniature city of Antwerp and the art museum were closed. We did enjoy the wide variety of people, the cathedral square, lace shops, and real Belgium waffles with whipped cream and fruit.

The kids were muttering, "Beach, beach," again so we headed for Oostende and found a crowded campsite. The manager directed us to park next to the main building, which housed the office, store, and restaurant that played loud music, because he said the ground was too soft for a heavy vehicle like ours. Soft ground or not, we decided to take our chances in the field where the other overnighters and tenters were camped. The ground felt hard as a brick. In the middle of the night we woke to the sound of pouring rain and imagined our motorhome sinking in to the axles and becoming a permanent fixture. The rain also woke a lot of tenters who carried on a heated discussion for an hour or so. In the morning we heard a sound like an ice cream truck. The kids were all excited till we saw the sign and realized it was hot soup. We only sank in an inch and hardly made any ruts when we left. We parked by a tram track with sand dunes and a beach on the west side till it began to mist, drizzle, sprinkle, and then pour.

Enough was enough. We headed back to Holland. We arrived in Delft and by the time we had finished after supper it had stopped raining, so we went for a walk beside a canal. There were some odd-looking birds swimming there and cozy little houses with lace curtains and flower boxes all along the sidewalk. The Porcelain Fles factory and sales room were interesting to see. A lady was painting a plate by hand with pigment which looked black but turned blue when fired. We picked out several small pieces in the seconds shop before heading to one of our favorite places, Madurodam. The miniature buildings, farms, canals, and other scenes were wonderful to see. Many parts of this miniature Holland are activated so we could see working locks, windmills, boats (even one that catches on fire and is extinguished by a fire patrol boat), cars, planes and many others.

From Madurodam it was only a short drive to the beach at the town of Scheviningen, which is completely unpronounceable but lovely to visit. Back near Rotterdam is the town of Gouda, known worldwide for cheese. We found a city parking lot. In the morning we joined the market crowd. The organ grinder played a tune as we visited the stalls of every imaginable kind of goods. Many of the sales people were clothed in traditional dress with heavy klompen on their feet. We watched a wooden shoemaker, a pewter smith, a cheesemaker, and people sealing the bargain and weighing cheese.

After buying fruit and cheese we headed back to the camper for lunch and a drive north to Marken and Volendam. They are towns on the Ijsselmeer which have retained their old-fashioned charm and ways of dress. While we were parked behind a restaurant in Volendam, the generator wouldn't stay on so we opened the hatch to see if we could find the problem. A Dutch family was parked there too and the dad and kids came over to see what was going on. It was quite a session with the two fathers and five kids all trying to get a peek. After scavenging a length of fan wire from a fan, the generator was put back into operation and we finished the laundry.

We stopped at the airport campground the next day to see if we could park our motorhome there over the winter and find a place to fix the refrigerator, generator, water pump and toilet (these had all begun to malfunction). We were not allowed to park there over the winter but we eventually found a camper storage place.

The next day we headed to a laundromat and spent about $60 to do ten loads of wash. We didn't get the last one dried but put it in our camper drier. Our generator wire came off so the drier quit on the way to Rotterdam. We parked by Solko's house again while we had a wonderful pizza dinner and got reacquainted with his two younger children, Solko Jr. and Claire, who had been in France the first time we came.

Up early the next morning, we packed all our backpacks and two large duffel bags (one had the wet laundry in it), cleaned up the motorhome inside, emptied the tanks, dropped Dave, Lois, Brian, Craig, Glenn, and Paul off by the airport train station, and took the motorhome to its winter parking spot. We filled the water lines and drains with antifreeze, covered the top half with a tarp, covered the tires, parked all nonfreezables by the furnace in the house, and were given a ride to the airport by the manager.

Dave had called a cheap hotel in Amsterdam and reserved two rooms. We parked the duffel bags in an airport locker and took the train to Central Station and a tram to the hotel. It had been four hours since Dave had called, and the desk clerk had given up on us and rented one room to someone else so we were faced with eight people in a room with four single beds. We decided that with some extra bedding and mattresses on the floor we wouldn't be any more cramped than in the motorhome.

A shower and a nap rejuvenated us enough to explore the city a little. We had a good dinner at a Chinese restaurant, walked by the Rijksmuseum and along the canals near the hotel. A tour in a canal boat was the first thing we did in the morning, followed by a visit to a diamond and jewelry center, the Mennonite church, a walk through the Begjin-hof (one of the first retirement centers and a lovely peaceful courtyard with a church where the pilgrims worshipped before going to England and America), and Madame Tussaud's Amsterdam Wax Museum. Anne Frank's house was a very interesting visit and (like good Minnesotans) we tried a Norwegian restaurant for supper where they had the biggest selection of fish I had even seen. We lived in semi-luxury that night with an additional room with three single beds.

Monday we foolishly tried the Rijksmuseum but it was closed so we rented pedal boats and paddled around the canals. We ate lunch at a restaurant/bakery and went shopping for toys and shoes. We fed the pigeons in Dam square. Brian and Elaine took the little boys to the hotel while Dave, Lois and I went for a walk around Central Station. We saw a lot of interesting people there: grannies, businessmen, ice cream vendors, street musicians, newspaper sellers, and some people using and selling drugs.

We bought tickets for the train the next day and took the tram to the hotel. We ate dinner at a pancake house near the hotel, took another walk and packed up ready to get an early start to the airport. When we got our bags out of the locker, the one with the damp laundry smelled awful and we felt sorry for the security people who go through luggage by hand. It was bad enough just to be near enough to carry it.

Our plane was late leaving Amsterdam and we found two other people assigned to the same seats as we were (it happened on all three flights that day) but we were such a large family they let us stay together. The flight from Boston was delayed due to tornadoes in the Minneapolis area but we were only a little late arriving in Rochester. Our friends, the Gambles, met us with balloons and welcome signs. In spite of the heat, it was good to be home.

(After three more summers we shipped the motorhome from Antwerp to Detroit and prepared for a trip to Alaska on the fiftieth anniversary of Al-Can Highway.)

Appendix II

Encounter with Depression*

by David Byer

My story would not be complete without including my encounters with depression. There may be a hereditary component here since I know several generations in my family in which one or more members suffered in this way.

My depression presented as an adjustment disorder, that is, it resulted from my attempts to deal with difficult events in my life. I know I had underlying symptoms at various points in my life. These really became apparent in May 1995 when I discovered marijuana plants being cultivated in our house. This was a real shock. Jeannie and I had never expected to encounter this. We had not anticipated that any of our children would use the weed.

My immediate response was one of grief and sadness. It seemed to me that I had lost my son to a culture I so much had wanted him to avoid. I was concerned about the effect my grief might have upon my work performance. I went to my immediate supervisor at Mayo Clinic, Dr. Steven Rettke, and discussed the issue with him. It seemed that I should be able to continue working. I asked Dr. Rettke to

---

*This account is included by the request of David Byer.

keep a close eye on me and let me know if I should take some time off from work.

After the initial shock, I adjusted fairly well until my son refused to accompany our family on a planned trip to Thailand. I canceled the trip for the two of us while the remainder of the family carried on. At that point I agreed to seek professional advice and started medication. This was helpful. Some people don't like the idea of consulting with psychiatrists and receiving medication. I do not share that feeling. I know of two people hospitalized in the early 1950s who did not have the benefit of modern medication. Their treatment consisted of administration of insulin to decrease their blood sugar until they convulsed. I am so thankful I was spared that barbaric treatment.

We knew very little about substance abuse. We participated in a counseling program. This was good for Jeannie and me. We had an opportunity to meet other parents who were dealing with similar situations. Many were single parents. Jeannie and I were glad we could go through this experience together with other parents.

In 1988, seven years prior to this, a sixteen-year-old Rochester youth murdered his parents and brother and sister. The murder instrument was an axe. This memory caused a lot of worry for both of us. We feared what might happen if a substance caused violence. I started keeping a journal describing what was going on. I detailed all the things we were doing. I wrote of our fears. My idea was that if something happened to us, the journal would bear witness to our compassion and care. I recently re-read the journal in preparation for this account. I had forgotten how frightened we were and the stressful times we experienced. The passage of time had smoothed my recollections.

We feared for the safety of our son. One of his friends, a neighbor, was a drug dealer. In June 1997, shortly after high school graduation, gang members murdered him. Dealing and using marijuana is not the harmless thing promoters would have us believe.

Several features of the depression stand out. I had a deep sense of failure as a father. I tried to discover what I should have done differently. I felt very guilty. Some well-meaning people have unhelpful ideas that depression is associated with unconfessed sin or a lack of faith, or worse. I couldn't see any relationship to my circumstance. I derived strength from my faith. Our church congregation was important to us. Jeannie and I were charter members. I had enjoyed serving in leadership roles.

About this time I heard a series of sermons on qualifications for church leaders. Although I may have misunderstood, I thought I should no longer occupy a leadership role in church. It seemed I did not have the respect of my children. I didn't see that as a disqualifier. However, I was certain some people in the congregation held that view. I didn't want to be put to a vote, so I removed myself from consideration.

It seemed odd that anger would occur in a depressed person. I experienced this to a greater degree than I care to admit. Another hallmark of depression—thoughts of suicide—were frightfully strong. As an anesthesiologist I had ready access to all sorts of medications. I had the knowledge of how to use them to guarantee a successful suicide. It would be so easy. However, as I considered it, I realized my suicide would merely compound our problems. I couldn't see leaving Jeannie alone. I loved her too much. I loved my children too much. What sort of witness of faith and hope would my suicide present to them?

I heard of Father Nick Mezacapa, Calvary Episcopal Church, Rochester, tell that he was called to the room of a patient who had just received some bad medical news. The patient asked, "What if I just ended it all?" Father Nick suggested it was difficult to place himself in the position of the patient. However, knowing the man and his family, Father Nick stated that the best gift for the family at this point could be to observe how the patient dealt with the bad news and lived out his life with dignity, honor and hope. The patient did so. These were good words for me.

I was encouraged by exchanges of email with a colleague, Dr. Michael Joyner. Here is an example from an email of August 1995: "Hang in there! You don't have to suffer alone. Everyone in the Department likes you and would do whatever they could to help, don't be afraid to reach out. You will find that almost everyone has had some really tough times, and that they are willing to share these with you. Mike." Dr. Joyner's advice to me is good advice for anyone dealing with depression.

I felt I had lost control over much of my life and my world. I began to look for something I could do that would make a difference. I was concerned about public safety. I volunteered to serve on our Mayor's Advisory Council on Neighborhood Associations. There was great interest in advancing public safety by forming neighborhood associations. I suggested we needed a booklet summarizing certain Rochester city ordinances. I initiated and participated in the writing of a booklet. Titled *Rochester: A Community of Friendly People & Active Neighborhoods*, it was intended to increase awareness of ordinances affecting neighborhoods. The booklet now is in its seventh printing and now bears the title *Ordinance Highlights: Guidelines for Neighborhood Awareness*.

In the interest of public safety, I also began reporting dead streetlights. I'm not sure this prevented any crime. However, it was an activity over which I had control. I derived some satisfaction driving down Broadway, our main street, and seeing all the street lights ablaze.

I was deeply offended by a conservative political activist whose Letter to the Editor claims that parents were primarily to blame for substance abuse in youth. I had experienced this sort of attitude. His letter provided an opportunity to tell my side of the story.

Jeannie and I dealt with substance abuse in our family household for at least six years. Two additional members were involved. I continued on medication. My depression diminished. When our church proposed building a youth and family center, Jeannie and I were enthusiastic supporters. This was something we could do on behalf of youth.

We had been deeply concerned that our family would be split up by the substance abuse or other issues. We are happy that we are on good terms with all of our children. We love them dearly. Two have told us there is nothing we could have done to prevent their involvement in substance abuse. They are all hard workers now and are self-supporting. Our six children enjoy getting together, especially if Dad is paying for a meal. Now we can relax and summarize our experiences with adolescents and recall that some of our children were low maintenance individuals; some were high maintenance.

Here are some final words about depression: Should I be depressed about the diagnosis of multiple myeloma received in April 2010? I have not been. I accepted it as our Lord's will for me. I have placed the matter in our Lord's hands. I am blessed by the excellent care I receive. I am blessed by world-wide prayer support on my behalf. An early cheerleader was one of my third cousins, Lela Hostetler. She has passed on. Encouragement has come in many other ways. On one day only, April 19, 2014, I felt really beaten down. I was recovering from a course of heavy chemotherapy. I had very painful sores in my mouth. I told my family I wasn't sure I could continue with the treatment plan. I had no strength left. I thought it might be time to discontinue treatment. I was certain that if I continued treatment, it would not be on account of my strength but because of strength provided by our Lord.

An answer came in less than twenty-four hours. An experienced nurse reviewed my course and indicated that I actually was doing much better than many patients: I had not required hospitalization for side effects. These comments provided the support I needed to continue forward. I believe our Lord inspired those words to me.

I have received regular visits from retired anesthesiologist Dr. Peter Southorn. These times have meant so much to me. Another colleague, Dr. Terese Horlocker, arranged for a Mass on my behalf at the Basilica of St. Francis of Assisi, Assisi, Italy. She also brought a crucifix from Jerusalem.

As of this writing I am enjoying the benefits of a second stem cell transplant. I feel I have a new lease on life. I keep busy because there are so many things I find to do. For example, I'm working on transcribing my grandmother's diaries. However, at only 100 days after transplant, the myeloma is progressing. The results lasted for a much shorter period than expected. I have told my physicians I feel better than I appear on paper. We haven't given up hope. We are busy pursuing the next possible steps in the treatment plan.

[Shortly after writing this account David died on November 7, 2014.]

Appendix III

Engaged Generosity:
David and Jeannie Byers' Sponsorship of Artworks in the Ruth E. Engle Memorial Collection of Children's Book Illustration

by Cherie Fieser*

As the Byers tell it, their involvement with the Ruth E. Engle Memorial Collection began with financial support and soon progressed to looking for illustrations to suggest for acquisition. Their immediate and genuine interest in the launching of such a collection is apparent in their actions following its announcement.

In December 2003, more than a year before the dedication of the Engle Memorial Collection, David visited the Kerlan Collection, the University of Minnesota's internationally known center of children's literature research. His interest in the Kerlan was piqued when he learned they recently acquired a number of E. B. Lewis[1] illustrations. The same day, he visited three bookshops in the Twin Cities.

---

*Cherie Fieser is Curator of the Ruth E. Engle Memorial Collection of Children's Book Illustration at Messiah College. In this engaging article she relates the acquisition and significance of some of the artwork in the collection (see photographs in the next section). The article also catches the always delightful relationship between her and the Byers. (EMS)

The following weekend, after attending a medical conference in New York, he visited more bookstores. He also stopped by the new Pediatric Emergency Department at the New York-Presbyterian Morgan Stanley Children's Hospital. That department incorporates vivid floor-to-ceiling illustrations from familiar children's books to help distract children and family members from stress and anxiety.

Believing he and Jeannie should be informed supporters of Murray Library's collection, David signed on as a Friend of the Kerlan. Saturday mornings thereafter, he arose before dawn and made the 85-mile trek to assist in digitizing their finding aids. He chose the letter L with authors and illustrators such as Madeleine L'Engle, Lois Lenski, and E. B. Lewis. One of Lewis's illustrations for *Talkin' About Bessie: The Story of Aviator Elizabeth Coleman*[2] by Nikki Grimes was the first artwork the Byers sponsored for inclusion in the Engle Memorial Collection in honor of Lydia and Mary E. Byer (see Fig. 1).

Soon David began attending children's literature conferences, lectures, and book award ceremonies. It wasn't long before he and Jeannie actively sought out galleries specializing in children's book illustration wherever they traveled—California, London, and Warsaw—and suggesting illustrations they were interested in sponsoring for the Engle Memorial Collection. Other times David wrote to illustrators directly to inquire about the availability of illustrations from a particular book.

David commented that he rather enjoyed "making suggestions and learning what the committee thinks. I haven't been shot down too many times!" He's right, of course; the selection committee enthusiastically embraced most of the Byers' suggestions—an indication of their engagement and discernment.

And wherever they went, they spread the word about the Engle Memorial Collection. David kept a list of institutions and people to whom he sent collection portfolios, frequently contacting me to say he "could use a few dozen more." Those who received portfolios often wrote to him to express their pleasure in learning about the collection and their wish to visit it. David sent a copy of one such letter, along with an enclosure about dandelions. "The seeds are carried away by the wind and travel like tiny parachutes," it read. "A strong wind can carry the parachutes miles away from the parent plant." At the top of the letter David jotted: "This just in.... I'll keep spreading dandelion seeds." It was an undertaking he would continue for the rest of his life.

When I mentioned to the Byers that the selection committee was considering the purchase of an illustration by Caldecott medalist Trina Schart Hyman for *Sense Pass King: A Story from Cameroon* by Katrin Tchana, David located a copy of the book at the Rochester Public Library (see Fig. 2). Because the artwork reminded him and Jeannie of the mission station at Macha in Zambia where they volunteered, they decided to sponsor the acquisition in honor of Jeannie's parents, Charles and Mary Alice Jordan. Hyman's sunlit painting of the detailed village setting became the second artwork the Byers funded for the collection.

On their annual trip to the mission station at Macha, David and Jeannie took along a copy of *Sense Pass King* to share with the children there. The children were captivated by the illustrations and the story. That experience led the Byers to develop a collection of illustrated children's books for the Vision Community Center Library at Macha Hospital—the only source of books at Macha.

David outlined this project in a presentation to the 30th International Board on Books for Young People (IBBY)[3] World Congress in Macau, China, 2006, which he attended to solicit advice and suggestions for further development of the Vision Community Center Library and to learn more about children's literature. He professed no expertise in children's literature in his presentation, but he did state his "intense interest in children, especially the children of Africa."

He made many interesting connections during his time at Macau: the curator-at-large for the collection of children's book illustration at the Israel Museum, Jerusalem; head of the Children's Literature Program at Srinakharinwirot University, Bangkok; coordinator of the 2006 Nami Island International Book Festival[4] in Korea. "The 2007 Nami Island festival would be a neat event," he related, and "the IBBY 2008 is in Copenhagen." As usual, he was setting his sights on future venues that would further inform his and Jeannie's involvement with the Engle Memorial Collection and "spread the word" about it.

As the Byers searched for new illustrations to sponsor, they were often guided by their areas of interest—women, people of color, people overcoming obstacles, Africa. And because they live from a global perspective, they were interested in sponsoring illustrations from around the world. This interest corresponded perfectly with the selection committee's criteria that the Engle Memorial Collection be international in scope, including illustrators from other countries as well as indigenous themes and folklore.

Not surprisingly, it was David who acquainted the selection committee with Africa Access[5], sponsors of the Children's Africana Book Awards (CABA), information he discovered on the U.S. State Department website. He saw the CABA event as a link to illustrators of African origin, such as Baba Wagué Diakité.

Later he met Harriet McGuire, a former foreign service officer in a number of African countries who also did media relations for CABA. He told her about the Engle Memorial Collection, his interest in Baba Wagué, and his and Jeannie's interest in Africa. Harriet shared the Byers' keen interest in children's book illustration and, intrigued by David's description of the Engle Memorial Collection, came shortly thereafter to see it firsthand.

That encounter provided contact information for Baba Wagué and David hastened to write of his interest in the illustrator's work. He and Jeannie knew the selection committee was interested in acquiring illustration styles not yet represented in the collection. There was no counterpart to Baba Wagué's dazzling illustrations—paintings on ceramic tiles, plates, and bowls as well as three-dimensional sculpture.

After suggesting that I communicate directly with Baba Wagué about pieces of interest, David said, "Just let me know when you need money and how much." Such a directive was not unusual since David often checked on the level of funds in the "Byer kitty"—particularly if a new acquisition was in the offing.

My conversation with Baba Wagué resulted in the acquisition of three stunning artworks from two books, one of which is *The Magic Gourd*, the 2004 CABA Honor book and winner of the Aesop Prize, conferred annually by the American Folklore Society upon English language books for children.

A brilliantly painted tile features the legendary trickster spider of Ghanaian folklore created for *The Pot of Wisdom:*

Ananse Stories (see Fig. 5). The Byers sponsored this piece in honor of Ghanaian physicians and friends, Drs. Lewis and Rosebud Roberts.

Children visiting the Engle Memorial Collection often respond with startled delight when they glimpse the large black insects painted inside *The Magic Gourd*'s ceramic bowl, but they are quickly drawn to the wonderfully quirky clay and stone chameleon sculpture from the same book which completes the trio (see Figs. 3, 4). These pieces honor Les and Celia Byer and grandchildren Vanessa Caffrey and Owen Byer.

In 2005, the Byers located an artwork by Australian illustrator Robert Ingpen for the Centenary Edition of *Peter Pan and Wendy* at a gallery in Victoria, Australia (see Fig. 6). Ingpen received the 1986 Hans Christian Andersen Award for Illustration and the Byers thought his work should be included in the Engle Memorial Collection.

"I think it might make a good investment to purchase this one," David wrote. "I'm enclosing a check which can be used for other purposes should [the selection committee] not choose to go after Jane." The selection committee chose to "go after Jane," however, and Ingpen's watercolor, "Jane Flies for Peter," soon made its way from the Melaleuca Gallery, Australia, to Murray Library at Messiah College. This acquisition honors David's parents, Everett and Adela Byer. End of story? Not quite.

One January morning three years later, I opened an email from David informing me that he and Jeannie were in London for the week. "Our first priority this morning was the Illustration Cupboard on Bury Street, not far from Picadilly Circus. There we saw a number of tempting children's book illustrations on display for their annual winter exhibition."

Among the temptations was a two-sided storyboard by Robert Ingpen for *Peter Pan and Wendy* which included an early thumbnail sketch for "Jane Flies for Peter"—the illustration already in the Engle Memorial Collection (see Fig. 7). Moreover, Ingpen's storyboard for this classic work was unusually detailed and included several thumbnail watercolors. An astonishing find, which the Byers offered to sponsor!

The storyboard not only demonstrates a particular aspect of the illustration process, but also further establishes the Engle Memorial Collection as a teaching collection.

Given their work in the medical field, the Byers were pleased to learn that Ingpen's illustrations for *Peter Pan and Wendy* were to be auctioned to raise money for the Barwon Health Foundation. Additionally, Ingpen arranged to donate all Australian royalties from the book toward redevelopment of the emergency department at the Geelong Hospital—the pediatrics area, in particular.

David and Jeannie sponsored purchase of the Ingpen storyboard in honor of Peter and Wendy Southorn. "This [dedication] represents our friendship with my anesthesiology colleague Peter, his wife Wendy, and their children," David explained.

> We first met them circa 1973 when he came from England for training at Mayo Clinic. Later when Jeannie and I were in London, I ran across Peter, one of the few of 8 million inhabitants I knew, in a medical bookshop near University College Hospital.... Although we are past 65 years of age, Peter and I continue to work at Mayo. His office is right next to mine.

When I commented on the numerous connections between the families and the surprising intersection of their paths, David shared yet another link.

Peter did a pediatric anesthesia fellowship at the Great Ormond Street Hospital for Sick Children. This hospital has the copyright to *Peter Pan and Wendy*. Great Ormond Street [Hospital] commissioned Ingpen to do the illustrations for the Centenary Edition.

And so it was that the Ingpen storyboard for *Peter Pan and Wendy* was dedicated to the Byers' friends, Peter and Wendy.

Holly Meade is one illustrator the Byers contacted directly. On a visit to Murray Library to see how the Engle Memorial Collection was progressing, they noted a copy of *Hush! A Thai Lullaby,* written by Minfong Ho and illustrated by Holly Meade, in a display unrelated to the collection. They "liked the cover and thought a Caldecott Honor artist should be represented."

After examining *Hush!* and other books Holly illustrated, David penned a note to Holly about the Engle Memorial Collection and his growing interest in children's book illustration. He asked whether any illustrations from *Hush!* and *Sky Sweeper* was on offer. "It would be nice for Cherie and her committee to have several Holly Meade illustrations to consider," he explained.

The selection committee voted unanimously to acquire Holly Meade's "Muddy Pig" spread from *Hush!* as well as a spread from *Sky Sweeper*, the latter notable for its "luminescent collage illustrations created from delicate Japanese papers" (see Figs. 8, 9).

Earlier, David mentioned that an illustration from *Hush!* "would honor our Thailand connections." Those connections included their Thai businesswoman friend, Morakot Rungkitwattanakul, and it is to her the Byers dedicated the piece. The *Sky Sweeper* spread honors Laura Heuton, sister-in-law to the Byers' daughter Elaine.

Soon after these artworks were installed as part of the Engle Memorial Collection, a message arrived from David:

> I'm putting some Thai items in the mail to you today. Firstly, there are two cushion covers. The fabric is typical of northern Thailand. Designed by our Morakot Rungkitwattanakul. Woven to her specifications by weavers in Nan province. Each bears her label Morakotphanan (Morakot from Nan)....
>
> Second, two menu ephemera from [Morakot's] Unique Thai restaurant in Los Angeles. She bought this restaurant sight unseen about 2 1/2 years ago....
>
> Third, not directly related to Morakot (Anne), but providing an example of northern Thailand hill tribe handicraft, is a colorful hat.

It was typical of David and Jeannie to surprise friends with gifts reflecting an intersection of interests or a shared enterprise. Later, I learned they had also sent Holly Meade two Thai pillow covers designed by Morakot. David shared Holly's thank you note because of her comments about the Engle Memorial Collection:

> I can't think what I did to deserve your gift but [it] was happily received! They are so striking...I instantly replaced my worn couch pillow covers with them, and felt like I had a new living room! Grateful.
>
> That an illustration from *Hush!* and *Sky Sweeper* are part of the Engle Collection is a source

of pride for me. My warm thanks again for making this possible.

Holly Meade's work played another role in the Byers' lives. Following David's diagnosis of multiple myeloma and the Byers' designation as "Splendid Friends" at *Friends of Murray Library*'s annual dinner meeting in 2010, a framed print by Holly Meade, "Prayers Going Up," was presented to the Byers in absentia and then sent to Rochester, MN. David's reaction upon opening the package follows:

> God has spoken in many ways in the past. Followers of Jesus know he continues to speak even in these days and in many ways. I never imagined that we would ever receive three Words From God delivered directly to our home via UPS Second Day Air at 17:05 on 15 OCT 2010.
>
> TODAY marks the SIXTH month since the multiple myeloma diagnosis on 15 APRIL. If there is anything to summarize Jeannie's and my experiences of the past six months it is "Prayers Going Up." I don't need to "go figure" why the parcel arrived today. I know. We are so thankful for "Prayers Going Up" at many places...from Ouagadougou, Burkina Faso [to] the Basilica of St. Francis, Assisi, Italy.
>
> I'm sure I'll have more to write. However, I do want this e-mail to go out with the date 15 OCT 2010.

Holly wrote, "It's a wonderful thing to witness (even from a distance) the loving support David receives. I'm honored that one of my prints has been chosen for such a gift." At the time, we didn't know that Holly had also battled cancer. Consequently, we were stunned and saddened to read of her death at 56 in June 2013.

Often the Byers' recommendation of an artwork not only matched the committee's selection criteria, but also had significant personal relevance. *The Hello, Goodbye Window* written by Norton Juster and illustrated by Chris Raschka is one such example (see Fig. 10). The book won the 2006 Caldecott Medal which is awarded annually by the American Library Association to the artist of the most distinguished American picture book for children. The Byers located the cover illustration for the book at a gallery in Los Angeles and hoped the selection committee would consider it.

The selection committee enthusiastically approved the acquisition of the Raschka illustration which the Byers dedicated to the memory of Choua Her and their times together. Beginning in 1984, the Byers became friends with a family of Hmong who had settled in Rochester, led from Laos to freedom by Choua Her, an unsung Hmong hero. Choua Her's twelve-year-old great niece, Boun Xou Her, became like a second sister to the Byers' daughter, Elaine, and spent many weekends with the family.

For the Byers, Raschka's illustration embodies fond memories of Choua Her who, though suffering from cancer, always came to the apartment's "hello-goodbye window" to wave goodbye to Boun Xou.

It would be hard to overstate the Byers' generosity. More than a few times I received a message from David saying, "I mailed a check the other day in case you need some money for illustrations under consideration." Even if he and Jeannie didn't have a specific artwork in mind, they wanted to ensure that a lack of funds would not prevent the committee from proceeding with a purchase.

One such gift made possible the purchase of three more artworks. Two of them are illustrations for *A Child's*

Christmas in Wales by two different illustrators (see Figs. 11, 12). These artworks allow viewers to see different approaches to illustrating the same text—not only the use of different media, but also what aspects of a story each illustrator chooses to depict. David and Jeannie sponsored these two pieces in honor of grandsons Owen, Grant, and Joshua Byer.

The third piece is a highly detailed watercolor of a Lakota warrior by English-born American author and illustrator Paul Goble for *The Woman Who Lived with Wolves & Other Stories from the Tipi* (see Fig. 13). A Caldecott medalist and recipient of the Library of Congress' Children's Book of the Year Award, Goble was adopted by Lakota Chief Edgar Red Cloud and was greatly influenced by Plains Indian culture.

David and Jeannie chose to honor Dr. Judith Salmon Kaur with the Lakota warrior illustration. Dr. Kaur has devoted her career to the improvement of survival rates for American Indians with cancer.

There seemed to be no end to the interfacing of the Byers' associations and acquaintances whether they suggested an artwork for the collection or the committee made the selection.

In November 2012, David and Jeannie traveled to London and Warsaw. A trip to London usually meant a visit to the Illustration Cupboard and the Byers were looking forward to an exhibit of illustrations by acclaimed British illustrator Angela Barrett.

> Our first stop today was at Illustration Cupboard. The first floor still had all the Barrett illustrations. We met John Huddy who informed us Barrett would be dropping by at 4 PM. Now we cool our heels in Fortnum and Mason Restaurant. I

have not energy to walk far. We likely will occupy this table for a while! I intend to meet Barrett.

Noting that the Illustration Cupboard was promoting some of Angela Barrett's earlier work as well as her most recent work, David proposed, "Perhaps Engle [selection committee] would like one of each to show earlier and most recent work?" As often as we experienced such generosity from the Byers, it never ceased to amaze me.

The selection committee identified a companion pair of Angela Barrett's paintings for *Joan of Arc* by Josephine Poole (see Figs. 14, 15). David and Jeannie were willing to have their recent gift to the collection fund the purchase and dedicated the pairing to Dr. Terese Horlocker, an anesthesiologist in Rochester, MN.

This recounting of the Byers' generosity and their pleasure in working with the selection committee to expand the Engle Memorial Collection only touches upon the amount of effort expended, connections made, and leads pursued. I will miss David's almost weekly communiqués alerting me to a new gallery or illustration, as well as family news, travels, and discoveries about whatever subject he was researching at the moment—a byproduct of his abundant curiosity.

Postscript

Following David's death in November 2014, *Friends* elected to add an illustration to the Engle Memorial Collection in his memory. While discussing possibilities with Jeannie, she mentioned how much she and David liked E. B. Lewis's illustrations for the Ethiopian folktale *Fire on the Mountain,* written by their mutual friend Jane Kurtz. "E. B. Lewis really captured Ethiopia in his illustrations," Jeannie said. "I can almost smell the eucalyptus fires!"

Jeannie's enthusiasm prompted me to contact E. B. Lewis and inquire about the availability of artwork from *Fire on the Mountain.* Lewis wondered why I was interested in work from that book, in particular.

I told him about the memorial for David, about his and Jeannie's love for Africa and its people, their service in Zambia and Ethiopia, their relationship with author Jane Kurtz whose parents were missionaries in Ethiopia the same time as Jeannie's parents, and more.

Then Lewis told me that the cover painting for the book was the only remaining artwork from *Fire on the Mountain* and, although he loaned the painting for exhibit, he never planned to sell it. Not only was it the first book he illustrated for children, but, more importantly, his editor told him that the author was moved to tears when she saw his illustrations for the book, so perfectly did they capture the Ethiopian landscape and the emotion of the tale.

Jane Kurtz's reaction to Lewis's illustrations for *Fire on the Mountain* sealed his decision to hold on to the cover painting titled "The Embrace" (see Fig. 16). He explained it with a favorite Mark Twain quotation: "The two most important days in your life are the day you are born and the day you find out why." Jane Kurtz's response to his work was his 'why.'

Suddenly the conversation took an unexpected turn. Lewis expressed his belief that things happen for a reason. Hearing about the Engle Memorial Collection, the Byers, and the significance the painting held for them, he said it seems the painting now belongs here as part of the collection. He was willing to sell it!

E. B. Lewis personally delivered his painting to Murray Library, committed to seeing its "new home." Jeannie, in true Byer fashion, flew from Minnesota for the event, joined by daughter Elaine and granddaughter Esther. The visit culminated with Lewis delivering a passionate and moving address to the selection committee, the *Friends'* Board and other members of the college, as well as education and art majors.

Because this illustration holds such meaning for David and Jeannie and reflects so many aspects of their lives, it will honor them both and their extreme generosity as patrons of the Ruth E. Engle Memorial Collection of Children's Book Illustration.

Endnotes

[1] Native Pennsylvanian Earl Bradley Lewis is the award-winning illustrator of more than 70 books for children. The Kerlan Collection purchased a set of original watercolors from Lewis's first 25 children's books.

[2] *Talkin' About Bessie* received the 2003 Coretta Scott King Book Award for Illustration. The Coretta Scott King Book Awards are given annually to outstanding African American authors and illustrators of books for children and young adults that demonstrate an appreciation of African American culture and universal human values.

[3] The International Board on Books for Young People is a non-profit organization which represents an international network of people who are committed to bringing books and children together.

[4] Nami Island hosted the first Nambook Festival in 2005 in celebration of the 200th anniversary of the birth of Hans

Christian Andersen. Since then, Nambook has earned an international reputation for its innovative and diverse approach to honoring the culture of children's books.

[5] Africa Access was founded in 1989 to help schools, public libraries, and parents improve the quality of their K-12 collections on Africa. The Children's Africana Book Awards are presented annually to the authors and illustrators of the best children's and young adult books on Africa published in the United States.

Appendix IV

Artworks in the Ruth E. Engle Memorial Collection
sponsored by the David and Jean Byer Family

* Specific artworks proposed by the Byers

FIGURE 1 * Watercolor by E. B. Lewis / 9" x 11.25"
TALKIN' ABOUT BESSIE: THE STORY OF AVIATOR ELIZABETH COLEMAN
by Nikki Grimes, 2002
Winner of the 2003 Coretta Scott King Illustrator Award
2004 gift in honor of Lydia and Mary E. Byer

198

FIGURE 2 Acrylic & ink illustration by Trina Schart Hyman / 20.25" x 9.25"
SENSE PASS KING: A STORY FROM CAMEROON by Katrin Tchana, 2002
2005 gift in honor of Charles and Mary Alice Jordan

FIGURE 3 Handmade polychromed
earthenware bowl
by Baba Wagué Diakité /
7.5" diam. x 4.5"
THE MAGIC GOURD: A WEST
AFRICAN FOLKTALE
retold by Baba Wagué Diakité, 2003
2007 gift in honor of
Les and Celia Byer

FIGURE 4 Hand-built clay & stone sculpture by Baba Wagué Diakité / 19" x 19.75" x 8"
THE MAGIC GOURD: A WEST AFRICAN FOLKTALE
retold by Baba Wagué Diakité, 2003
2007 gift in honor of Vanessa Caffrey and Owen Byer

FIGURE 5 * Handmade polychromed earthenware tile
by Baba Wagué Diakité / 11.75" x 11.5"
THE POT OF WISDOM: ANANSE STORIES by Adwoa Badoe, 2001
2007 gift in honor of Lewis and Rosebud Roberts

FIGURE 6 * Watercolor by Robert Ingpen / 8.25" x 10.25"
PETER PAN AND WENDY by J. M. Barrie, Centenary Edition, 2004
2005 gift in honor of Everett and Adela Byer

FIGURE 7 * Watercolor, pencil & ink two-sided storyboard
by Robert Ingpen / 16.5" x 11.5"
PETER PAN AND WENDY by J. M. Barrie, Centenary Edition, 2004
2008 gift in honour of Peter and Wendy Southorn

FIGURE 8 * Cut paper & ink illustration by Holly Meade / 21" x 12.5"
HUSH! A THAI LULLABY by Minfong Ho, 1997 Caldecott Honor Book
2008 gift in honor of Morakot Rungkitwattanakul

FIGURE 9 Japanese paper & ink collage by Holly Meade / 26" x 17.75"
SKY SWEEPER by Phillis Gershator, 2007
2008 gift in honor of Laura Heuton

FIGURE 10 * Mixed media illustration by Chris Raschka / 22.25" x 13"
THE HELLO, GOODBYE WINDOW by Norton Juster, Winner of the 2006 Caldecott Medal
2008 gift in memory of Choua C. Her

FIGURE 11 Wood engraving by Fritz Eichenberg / 12" x 9"
A CHILD'S CHRISTMAS IN WALES by Dylan Thomas, 1969
2011 gift in honor of Owen Byer

FIGURE 12 Gouache, ink & torn paper illustration by Chris Raschka / 10.5" x 6.5"
A CHILD'S CHRISTMAS IN WALES by Dylan Thomas, 2004
2011 gift in honor of Grant and Joshua Byer

FIGURE 13 Gouache, watercolor & ink illustration by Paul Goble / 7" x 9.75"
THE WOMAN WHO LIVED WITH WOLVES & OTHER STORIES FROM THE TIPI
told by Paul Goble, 2010
2011 gift in honor of Dr. Judith Salmon Kaur

206

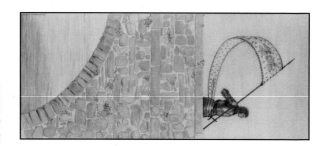

FIGURES 14, 15 Gouache illustrations by Angela Barrett / 4" x 9.75" (L); 10.5" x 9.75" (R)
JOAN OF ARC by Josephine Poole, 1998
2013 gift in honor of Terese Horlocker

FIGURE 16 ✳ Watercolor by E.B. Lewis / 10.5" x 13.5"
FIRE ON THE MOUNTAIN
by Jane Kurtz, 1994
Gift of *Friends of Murray Library*, 2015
In honor of David and Jeannie Byer, Splendid Friends
and generous patrons of the Ruth E. Engle Memorial Collection

Detail of the Ruth E. Engle Memorial Collection of Children's Book Illustration on the lower level of Murray Library, Messiah College. More illustrations in the collection are featured on the first floor gallery.

The Ruth E. Engle Memorial Collection of Children's Book Illustration now includes more than 40 original illustrations created for children's books—more than can be displayed at one time—and is expanded annually. A copy of the book for which each illustration was created is also on view; additional copies of the books are in Murray Library's juvenile literature collection and may be checked out.

The Engle Memorial Collection includes illustrators from seven countries, an impressive variety of illustration techniques, and an extensive array of styles and subjects. The collection may be viewed during regular library hours, free of charge.